Poetic Justice

Poetic Justice

A collection of poems, prose, and songs consisting of topics about everyday life and ordinary people.

J. D. Jackson

Writers Club Press
San Jose New York Lincoln Shanghai

Poetic Justice
A collection of poems, prose, and songs consisting of topics about
everyday life and ordinary people.

Writers Club Press
an imprint of iUniverse, Inc.

For information address:
iUniverse, Inc.
5220 S. 16th St., Suite 200
Lincoln, NE 68512
www.iuniverse.com

ISBN: 0-595-23508-5

Printed in the United States of America

Contents

Contents

Preface

Have you ever really taken a close look at people as you go about your day to day activities? When they passed by you, did you ever wonder what their lives would be like had they taken a different path? As I was sitting around one day enjoying the peace and solitude, the words, **if only**, kept coming to mind. It's as if the people were saying to themselves, if only I hadn't robbed that woman, if only I'd said yes to that job offer, if only I'd gone to college, or, if only I'd married…just to list a few. As I started to write down a few notes, the words started to flow and before I knew it, I had written, **If Only**.

From that one effort, the idea for this book was born. As a word, phrase, person, or a certain event came to me, I would jot down a few notes. Over the months to follow, I had written over one hundred pieces. Poetry, prose and songs can tell us stories that each of us can relate to in one way or another. Each individual poem or song has meaning that can touch the hearts of those that read or listen to the words. As you read, you may come to realize that through poetry we can truly describe the experiences of living.

Take the first step. Take the time to read the first poem that grabs your attention. The satisfaction you get from reading that one poem will probably lead you to read the others. They are without doubt some of the most interesting subjects you've seen in quite some time. The emotional response you exhibit will vary depending on your relationship to the piece and according to your own personal life and beliefs. If done properly, many of you will shed some tears and maybe even share a good laugh or two. Hopefully, though, many others will think long and hard about the topics being discussed. If they really hit home and get to your inner-being, then maybe you'll think twice about that pending break-up, lost love, or maybe about the loved one who died recently.

Look at and enjoy the humor of **Grandma** or **Con Man**. Have you been thinking about cheating on your spouse or do you think that possibly your spouse has been cheating on you? Then look at **Long Haul Driver**. Have you lost someone recently due to old age or illness? Then you will enjoy reading **Memories of You** or **The Last Good-bye**. If you've been blessed with a child, consider the pain and grief of the mother talked about in **Little Girl Lost**.

Although not intentional, I've managed to include subject's that each of us can relate. They include humor, adventure, true life, marital relations, family, friends, politics, religion, memory's, history, war, life, death, personal choices, love, fear, insecurity, crimes and criminals, vanity, happiness and others. Collectively, we are the subjects of these pieces, and individually, we are the only ones who can stop the cycle mentioned in a few. The **inspiration** for each piece is clearly noted in order to take the guesswork out of the equation. I felt it necessary to include the event or person in order to give the reader just a little insight as to their origin. Taking the advice of teachers and professors I've met over the years, each one is based on a life experience in one way or another. As a collection, they were written about people I've met during my life, a person or group of people I've read about, or a particular thing or an event I've experienced at some point during my life. If you just let yourself go, it's easy to experience the emotions that each one is intended to invoke.

I truly enjoyed writing each one and am very thankful for all the memories I've retained over the years. I pray that you will enjoy reading them as much as I enjoyed putting them on paper.

Read them—think long and hard about them—but most of all, enjoy them.

Thank you,

J. D. Jackson

Acknowledgements

To my wife, for all of the many sacrifices she's had to make over the years and for standing by me through thick and thin. To my family, friends, neighbors, acquaintances, and to all the unknowns for their **inspiration**. To Hazel King, Heritage Bible College, for her editing and helpful comments. To my God, for giving me the abilities to do the many things I can do. Without His help and all of the memories provided me over the years, none of this would have been possible.

Inspiration

To all those individuals who have ever said to themselves or to another person; **if only** I'd stayed in the military or **if only** I'd married such or such. This one is to all the **if only's** of this world.

If Only

Our love was forever, this we just knew.
And in the beginning we both said, "I do."
You were always around me; oh, how I loved you.
What God joined together would always be true.

We lived and we prospered; we had everything.
A home and a family, a sweet song to sing.
We traveled the land; oh, what sights to see.
But we never thanked God for letting it be.

As time took its toll, we just drifted apart.
Something was missing we had from the start.
Fingers were pointed and some words were said.
Somehow we both knew our marriage was dead.

The love we once had was taken away
By the one who wanted to party and play.
Had God remained first in our hearts,
We'd still be together as from the start.

If only I'd called when I needed him most;
If only I could have seen.
If only I'd prayed to the heavenly host,
None of this would have been.

If only to have one last chance
To make things right with him.
I know I could put the love and romance
Back in our hearts again.

—J. D. Jackson

Inspiration

Us, the children of God. Were it not for Him, none of this would exist. So let Him know how happy and pleased you are for having a chance at life.

Children of God

Children of God, that's who we are,
Staying close to Him, never straying too far.
Children of God, that's all we want to be,
Standing up for Him for the whole world to see.

Children of God, from sea to shinning sea.
Devil does his best, but we get the victory.
Children of God, always shouting His name,
Watching Satan run, and he'll never be the same.

Children of God, we'll never walk alone.
Jesus came to earth to take us to our home.
Children of God, we have no sins today.
The blood of Jesus Christ has washed them away.

Children of God, we're all the same to Him.
Doesn't matter a bit if we're short, tall, fat, or thin.
Children of God, we pray to Him each day
To save our mortal soul, make sure we never stray.

—J. D. Jackson

Inspiration

This piece was written after the events of September 11, 2001. Even though it was written for those who left home that morning and never returned, it is timeless and could apply to similar situations even today.

Memories of You

As we travel through this life living it from day to day.
Memories keep building up we've experienced along the way;
But it's not until we need them that we pull them out to see,
Right or wrong, good or bad, they're all special to me.

I can still remember the day he made me his friend and wife,
And how excited I truly was when I became a part of his life.
I remember that he loved me and I remember our first kiss.
I remember Mama talking to me about special days like this.

I remember the vows I made to him which came from the heart,
To love, honor and cherish him, 'til death do us part.
I remember the grin he had when he would look at me and stare.
I remember his soft, gentle touch and the way he parted his hair.

I remember all the fun we had on the trip we took last year,
And the special feeling I got when he took away my fear.
I remember at night how nice it was to see his smiling face,
And how angry I'd get when he told me to give him space.

I can remember him waiting until he got his kiss by the door,
But now my memories come to an end, never to be anymore.
For on this day an angel of God came down to take him home,
And left me here with my memories so I would never be alone.

Some memories give us hope, while others we question why.
And some of them will stay with us while others slowly die.
Memories are there to build on as we take life step by step.
Memories are a gift from God; this we should never forget.

Personal Memories and Notes

Our memories of all the good times or memories of the bad
Can bring us needed laughter or make us feel real sad.
Memories can sustain us during trying times like these,
And memories can even build us up or bring us to our knees.

—J. D. Jackson

Inspiration

This country apparently doesn't like to toot its own horn. It's a good place to live and the Lord knows there's a lot that could change to make it even better. Those of us born and raised in this country had a dream as children, or for some, as adults. For those coming here to join us, the dream still exists and can be realized with goals and good old hard work—The American Dream. It's out there: go get it.

The American Dream

America was born during a time of trouble.
We were seeking peace and a place to pray.
Oh, how we've fought and how we've struggled;
To keep our freedoms for another day.

Our people came from different countries,
They left their homes and way of life.
They brought their dreams and determinations
And they got it done without the strife.

America's doors are always open
That's what it means to live and be free.
If called to fight, many would answer
Just to protect the American Dream.

When famine strikes those far-off lands,
America's there just to lend her hand.
We give from the heart to those in need,
We're second to none always taking the lead.

America's there for the world to see
Just what it means to live and be free.
We've stood the time and passed every test,
And we're always alert and at our best.

Let freedom ring throughout this country.
Let freedom ring throughout the land.
We'll live or die to defend our freedom.
With the help of God, we'll make our stand.

—J. D. Jackson

Inspiration

Good or bad, some of us daydreamed as young children
and even into adulthood. There's a very different world
hiding there in the privacy of your mind. Go there from
time to time and enjoy it. Reality can always wait. Just
don't forget to come back to this one.

Garden In My Mind

When life knocks me down
And takes away my hopes and dreams,
Everything I've ever worked for
Is destroyed, or so it seems.

But on any given day of the week
I can always steal away
And return to that garden in my mind.

It's there that I can see
Some things that may never be,
Like a house on a hilltop
That was built for you and me.

Yes, I know you love me so
And I know you really care,
But that's only in the garden in my mind.

As I sit here by the willow tree
Listening to the birds and the bees,
I am thrilled and ever so happy
About the news I just received.

There'll come a day not too far away
When pure love prevails,
But that's only in the garden in my mind.

There's a garden in my mind
That I visit from time to time,

Personal Memories and Notes

Just to think about the things
That might have been.

That garden is the only place
That's fit for the human race.
Where peace, love and harmony abound.

—J. D. Jackson

Inspiration

Contrary to what some people tend to believe, things in this world do matter to us. Many people turn their heads and choose not to get involved. Listen up, if you continue to ignore the things going on around you, they will usually end up controlling you. Look, pay close attention and react accordingly.

What Does It Matter?

What does it matter where the winds do blow
Since we're also looking for the right place to go?
When the sky looks nasty and the clouds are black,
Always remember to keep the winds at your back.

And what does it matter if the sun shines or not?
Has no effect on giving and life can't simply stop.
By giving to those who are hungry or oppressed,
A life may be saved to become that country's best.

And what does it matter if we have eyes to see?
Of the entire universe, this is the best place to be.
Whether it's by sight, smell, or touch of the hand,
I'd much rather be here than in some distant land.

And what does it matter if we live free today?
Without true resolve, it can be taken away.
Simply ignore the signs and keep turning your back.
Your freedoms are lost and evil picks up the slack.

And what does it matter if we have ears to hear?
Just listening to the truth can give us reason to fear.
We must act on the messages we receive each day.
So the price of freedom we will never have to pay.

We need the winds to keep fresh the air,
And we need the sun to bring warmth to bear.
We need eyes to separate the good from the bad,
And we need ears to distinguish happy sounds from the sad.

Personal Memories and Notes

We need to understand these things one by one,
That our freedoms were paid for by the blood of our sons.
So what does it matter? We may ask time and again.
If we lose these things, we're looking at the end.

For what good is man without these gifts from God?
Just ignore the evil, and it'll control you with the rod.

—J. D. Jackson

Inspiration

While working one of the many jobs held over the past years, I started thinking of those around me. Believe it or not, some convicts love their existence, while others hate each and every day of incarceration. But there are a few who have no clue whatsoever. This silly and comical piece came to mind one morning as I was thinking about those with no clue whatsoever.

Con Man

Sold some marijuana and they threw me in the can.
But it did 'em no good 'cause I'm still called the man.
I'm known all over this beautiful little camp.
If you need to make a deal, you're talking to the champ.

It seemed like the right thing to do at the time.
Never knowing the judge was going to give me mine.
The man gave me twenty for selling my stuff.
Never imagined prison life was going to be this rough.

If you lay out of work and your funds are running low.
Homeboy will tell you just where you need to go.
I deal for tobacco; I deal for the weed,
I deal for the junk or anything you need.

'Cause I'm the con man, just a con man, a plain and simple,
        little con man.

My woman said she was going to wait on me,
Long before she knew what the sentence would be.
Didn't take her long though to change her little plan;
Told me first visit she done found another man.

Making plans for the future and things are looking good.
Had my time reduced 'cause I'm doing what I should.
Got some land I bought just south of Tijuana.
A prime location for a crop of marijuana.

I served my time and followed through with my plan.
The man bought my weed and threw me back in the can.

Personal Memories and Notes

Took me back to the court and made example of me.
They gave me fifty years and threw away the key.

'Cause I'm the con man, just a con man, a plain and simple,
    little con man.

—J. D. Jackson

Inspiration

If you were to try everything you could to please that special someone and still got slapped down, wouldn't you want to know why? Sure, it's important to know why to some of life's problems. At other times, though, knowing the answer could cause you more grief than those times you are just left wondering. These are choices we make as we live and die.

Why

I worked all my life to make a good home for you,
Gave you everything I had and look at what you do.
You took away the reasons I had to carry on.
You stopped loving me and destroyed our little home.

I've never loved anyone the way I've loved you.
Can't stand another day even if you say we're through.
And tomorrow may bring a new love to my life,
But I'll never forget the day that I made you my wife.

Tell me what to say to our kids late at night.
If they ask for their mom, or did we have a big fight?
Will their sorrow and tears ever go away?
Even when they realize you've gone away to stay.

You followed your dreams and left the old life behind.
Forsaking your family, our life, and the time.
You grew tired of being their mom and my wife,
And left it all behind just to start your new life.

Why, oh why, did you take things this far?
Why did you give up on us?
Why couldn't you figure out who you are
And avoid all of this fuss?

—J. D. Jackson

Inspiration

Feelings. You know the feelings you have for a certain person, but the trick is to find out how the other person feels about you. Somewhere along the way, feelings should be expressed. The simple approach has often worked for many people. The response you get is either a yes or a no. Simple and directly to the point. If the answer is yes, people tend to act silly, and some act downright giddy; life is good. Then you wake up, because your life is just beginning. Ah-love, isn't it great?

Give Your Love To Me

You can call me selfish if you really need to.
My sole reason for living is to love and cherish you.
Whatever I try, I can't get you off my mind,
Can't imagine being without you not even for a time.

Diamonds are forever, as my love is for you.
It was a match made in heaven for just us two.
I've waited many years for you to come to me,
So don't argue with fate; just let your life be.

I'll make all your days so serene and carefree.
Like floating on a soft white cloud over a calm blue sea.
And I'll fill all your nights with joy and happiness.
Like a never-ending wedding day that's sealed with a kiss.

You know that I love you and I speak from my heart.
I'll stand by you forever and we'll never part.
And for all these things that are meant to be,
I'll make it all happen, just give your love to me.

Won't you listen to me, darling,
And consider what's to be?
Don't fight your inner feelings;
Just give your love to me.

—J. D. Jackson

Inspiration

A Catholic priest I served with many years ago. Actually, I met the man while the two of us were trying to help this country fight a war in Vietnam during the years, 1966-1967. We were both stationed in Chu Lai, Vietnam, at the time, and I decided to listen to him preach one Sunday. It was a very hectic time as you can understand, and one day he was gone. A year or so later, I read all about what happened to him in the Stars and Stripes. It's not every day a priest receives this country's highest award, the Medal of Honor. Is it possible that I'm here today because of coming in contact with him? Could be, but I'll never know for sure. It's a good thought nevertheless.

Man Of the Cloth

Capadano was a man of the cloth who was called away to war.
But little did he know at the time, he would never see home
    anymore.
The duties of a man called by God is to save every lasting soul
And to give comfort, peace and salvation as he crawls from
    hole to hole.

He was ordered to report to Vietnam in the fall of '66,
Set up his business in a chapel by the sea made of stone, wood
    and sticks.
As sailors and marines came calling, he was doing the work of
    God,
And it wasn't too long after I met the man that he once again
    got the nod.

Sent to the field to be with his men as they fought the enemy
    up close,
He wept, cried and prayed to God every time they tied a tag
    to some toes.
The men around him kept falling as the enemy rained down
    its fire,
And Capadano kept on giving last rites or words meant to
    inspire.

A shot from the enemy found him, but he continued helping
    his men
As more shrapnel and bullets struck him, he still refused to
    give in.
One marine after another was saved by him that day,
And as he continued the work of God, his life finally slipped away.

Personal Memories and Notes

Capadano was a man of the cloth who was called away to war,
And on his final trip back home, he had something he'd never
    worn.
The Congressional Medal of Honor was presented to him
    that day,
And the memory of him will remain with me until I too am
    taken away.

Capadano was a man of the cloth that was called away to war...

—J. D. Jackson

Inspiration

Our greatest resource—the kids. When will today's parents come to realize that they and they alone are responsible for the safety of their children? Yes, it's so much easier to send them to the toy section while you shop. There's one very important problem with that situation you need to keep in mind. Some freak out there wants your child as a play toy. Are a few moments of peace worth a lifetime of torment?

Little Girl Lost

She was born on the south side of Boston
To a family that had everything.
Blonde hair, blue eyes, a cute little grin
And a voice that could really sing.

As the little girl grew from diaper to dress,
She filled her heart with love.
And touched the lives of family and friends.
Was pure as a snow-white dove.

She had her choice of toys and things,
And would always share them with friends.
But the values she learned over her short life
Couldn't help her in the end.

She and her mom went shopping one day
Just to buy some clothes and supplies.
Looking forward to starting school real soon
And knowing her, that's no surprise.

While she and her mom stood in line
To pay for her new things.
Mom turned away to greet a new friend
That she was taking under her wing.

And during that one brief moment,
The little girl just walked away.
Being coaxed outside by a stranger
She was to meet her God that day.

Personal Memories and Notes

Because love and trust is a natural thing
To a beautiful child of God;
But when that trust is used and abused
It usually takes just a nod.

—J. D. Jackson

Inspiration

In the words of one simple individual from the state of California, "can't we all just learn to get along with each other?" Or something like that. Anyway, it's just not going to happen. It's unfortunate, but a simple fact of life. Because of that fact, we must send our people out to defend and protect our way of life. Contrary to what some think about our Armed Forces, they are—Heroes All.

Heroes All

You were on my mind last Sunday
And throughout the holidays.
I couldn't shake this queasy feeling
Or my desire to kneel and pray.

Many families will come together
During this festive time of the year.
Many others will miss their loved ones
Little children will shed some tears.

Our fathers, sons, and daughters
Were called away to war
To defend our rights and freedoms,
Keep us safe forever more.

And as you and several others
Sat quietly talking one day,
I was to understand much later
My desire to kneel and pray.

Around six o'clock that evening
As the day came slowly to an end,
A rocket landed near you,
Killing them and my best friend.

I will always love and miss you
Throughout the coming years.
If you can visit me this Sunday,
You will see me cry some tears.

Personal Memories and Notes

Love between a man and a woman
Can always be taken away.
So try to cherish each waking moment
And remember to kneel and pray.

—J. D. Jackson

Inspiration

Once again, I drifted back to the events of September 11, 2001. What kept going through my mind was that thousands of memories about these people would now come to an end. The last thing they heard, the last event attended, or the last visual picture of a particular loved one was now frozen in their memories. Those lost on that particular day would forever be remembered just the way they were. Their faces, sounds, expressions, etc. were now forever frozen in time.

Frozen In Time

As I sit by my window on these long and lonely nights,
I think about the times when you held me oh so tight.
Even though I've lost something special of mine,
I still have these memories that are frozen in time.

I thank you for the fun we had and I thank you for your smile.
I thank you for your charm and grace and for going the
       extra mile.
I thank you for loving me and for being ever so kind,
And I thank you for the memories that are frozen in time.

I'm the only one to blame, my dear, for throwing it all away,
And I'm sure we'd be together still if I hadn't left you that day.
I told you my sad story in a letter I left behind.
At least I have my memories that are frozen in time.

You belong to another and I could never destroy your home.
You worked hard to build your family and I chose to be alone.
He gets to enjoy your beauty every day the sun does shine,
And all I have are my memories that are frozen in time.

So once again I'll sacrifice this love I have for you.
By leaving this town one last time just to start my life anew.
As the years pass slowly by, I'll get you out of my mind.
And the memories I have of you should fade away with time.

—J. D. Jackson

Inspiration

Love is worldwide. Some are so madly in love they make it a point to remember every time and location they see the person of their affections. Because of shyness or low self-esteem, they just never step forward to relay their feelings to this other person. As a result, love is lost. Go back and try again. What if this special someone actually said yes? However, don't cross the line and stalk the person; and, lastly, no means no. If that's the answer, get a life and move on.

I Saw You

I saw you strolling on the seashore.
I knew right then you were for me.
I love that side of a woman,
Never afraid to let it be.

I saw you crying at the movies.
The romantic side of you was clear.
Love abounds in a woman,
Not afraid to get too near.

I saw you walking in the park,
Watching all the kids at play.
I admire that in a woman,
And I hope it's with you to stay.

I saw you leaving church on Sunday,
Just as pretty as you could be.
It takes a special kind of woman,
Just to stay with a man like me.

I saw you standing at the altar,
With a stranger on your arm.
I never knew you loved another;
I just let him steal your charm.

Words of Inspiration

A wise man will hear, and will increase
    learning;
And a man of understanding shall attain
    unto wise counsels.

Proverbs 1:5

I saw you riding with your family,
Just the other day at three.
And it makes me feel so angry
That you got away from me.

There's a moral to this story
Every man should learn to heed.
When you find the perfect woman,
There's no excuse for lack of speed.

Find a way to express your feelings
And let her know that you're aware.
If she shows the slightest interest,
You'll know you're almost there.

But if you fail to let her know this,
Someone else will steal her heart.
And if you fail to heed my story,
Your two lives will surely part.

So go and tell her that you want her,
And let her know you really care.
Then tell her that you love her,
And that you'll always be there.

—J. D. Jackson

Inspiration

Ok, stop already—it was Christmas and I heard that silly song once again. I just had to try and stop the rumor from spreading any further. It's not true; grandma was not in the area at the time. She lives. Grandma is alive and kicking. Yes. Oh, ok—sorry, I got carried away.

Grandma

So much has been said about Grandma,
But everything you've heard is not true.
She's been around these parts for ages
And there's nothing that she can't do.

It's time to put an end to this rumor,
And you'll believe when you see her smile.
It wasn't Grandma who got hit that evening
Those reindeer missed her by a mile.

Now many say Grandma's a looker,
And she went shopping for something new.
She was invited to a party this evening
And she can still turn a head or two.

Grandma is the one with the answers.
She's never afraid to tell you the truth,
And if you want to catch up on gossip,
You visit her and not a psychic's booth.

God bless each and every grandma.
And we pray that none will ever fall.
And in spite of all their meddling,
We love them dearly, one and all.

—J. D. Jackson

Inspiration

That love thing again. It just doesn't ever go away, does it?
Same old story, one person madly in love with another.
Wants to know the answer to a question and they're
waiting by the phone. So call already, they're waiting
patiently. Go—call.

Do You Ever Think About Me?

I would go to the ends of the earth for you,
Or could easily give up an arm.
I would sacrifice every thing for you,
Just to win over your charm.

A person like you doesn't come along
But once in a blue moon.
And I know I'll lose my only chance
If action isn't taken real soon.

I've thought about the things we could do,
And the places we could go.
I've thought about some names for our kids,
Provided you make it so.

I've thought about the mom you could be,
Or a career, if that's what you choose.
I've thought about the life we could have
And I'm sure we would never lose.

I know I've said the right things to you
And have told you what I'd like to see.
As I wait patiently by the phone, I wonder—
Do you ever think about me?

—J. D. Jackson

Inspiration

I started thinking about a song heard many years ago about a character named Big John, Jim, Joan or something like that. Anyway, as the words came forth, they slowly changed into **Old Joe**. A man with plenty of sense, both common and learned, and knew there had to be something better in life than a large mortgage, a big car, long hours and a large salary. Well Joe found it, and loved what he found. So let your emotions go, life allows us to do things like that. Besides, the Old Joe's of this world would appreciate it.

Old Joe

Joe was a big kid for a child of seven
And always seemed to be out of place.
He took honors when he left college
And went out to join the rat race.

Joe left home and headed for the city
In search of the milk and honey.
He realized as the years passed by
There's more to life than just the money.

For a man to be a man, he needs to find a place
Where he thinks he can do the most good.
And as time passed him by, Old Joe realized
He wasn't doing what he knew he should.

Joe left the city then headed back home,
Forsaking his lifestyle and the pay.
He found a job pushing a mop and broom
Never regretting it, even to this day.

Year after year he would steer the kids
Away from the streets and the crime.
By listening to them as they came to school
And giving them a little of his time.

Old Joe influenced so many young kids
And he knew he'd done the right thing.
He always smiled as he reminisced
And just worked until he heard the bell ring.

Personal Memories and Notes

When Joe was finally laid to rest,
There wasn't a soul left in town.
Thanks to his kids, both old and new
Everything in town had closed down.

For a man to be a man he needs to find a place,
Where he thinks he can do the most good.
And as time passed by, Old Joe realized
He was doing what he knew he should.

—J. D. Jackson

Inspiration

I'm country, born and raised, and proud of it. I'm also good and happy, so what else can be said? Country folk are just that way.

Country Folk

The sun shines bright in the country,
And the moon shows the way at night.
When we see the stars in their glory,
We know everything is all right.

When you live way out in the country,
Far away from the bustling crowd.
The smells will touch your senses
And the sounds are never too loud.

People are moving to the country,
Looking for a new way of life.
And men are staying in the country,
Hoping to find a country wife.

Country wives are one of a kind
And they'll take good care of you.
Just show them that you love them,
And there's nothing they won't do.

Country folk love living free
And country folk love to dance.
Country folk are good and neighborly
And country folk love to romance.

Country folk take care of themselves
And country folk know how to live.
Country folk work hard every day
And country folk know how to give.

—J. D. Jackson

Inspiration

My neighbor. The man just doesn't know how or when to stop. Always coming and going to or from whom knows where. A very good, happy and dedicated man. Yes, he's a country preacher, or maybe a town preacher. Well, he's definitely not a city preacher.

The Preacher

The preacher left home this morning,
On his way to comfort a friend.
Seems like the work of a preacher
Is the type that will never end.

He fills the church every Sunday morning
The people just love to hear him talk.
It's rare to find him behind the podium
Because he like's to be out front to walk.

He preached today with love and conviction,
Then found some time for his wife.
And later in the day he preached a funeral
For a friend who had lost his life.

You'll find him working both day and night
At a home or a hospital room.
And when he finds a quiet moment or two,
He'll finish a sermon to be given soon.

He feels our joys and feels our pain, and
Gets real pleasure from hearing the choir sing.
He'll bless your child, anoint your head, and do
All that he can to introduce you to the King.

You see him on the streets talking to friends, and
You can see him in church talking about our sins.
If he's leaving home going to who knows where,
He's doing God's work because he really cares.

—J. D. Jackson

Inspiration

At one time or another, we were all teenagers. That's a given and since we have firsthand knowledge of what they go through, we should be able to help them, right? Yea, right. The pressures are apparently greater on the teens of today, and the help from some mothers and fathers has gone in the other direction. Those who still have hands-on experience with their kids are to be recognized for some type of achievement award. Seriously, years from now you teens will learn that the older you get, the smarter your parents become. And I bet that many years from now, you end up appreciating every thing they ever tried to do for you. So stay home, and have a good life. Running away only creates additional problems for you and everyone involved.

The Runaway

Your mama and daddy treated you real good,
Showed you real love and did everything they could
To protect you—from the evil of this world,
And watched over you—their sweet little girl.

It didn't matter to them how busy things would get,
They always found a way to be there for you; yet
You never saw—the things they did for you
As you grew—you felt loved and just knew

That your mom and dad would take care of you,
And to do every thing to make sure you grew
To be a woman—to be loved and their pride and joy
And a mother—of her own little girl or boy.

When you turned sixteen things seemed to change.
You turned to drugs and then had to exchange
Your own body—for the money and the drugs, and
You gave up—on all their love and hugs.

Early one morning we heard a knock at the door,
And your father went down and saw the four
Just standing there—they had that look on their face
And they told him—just how you'd lost your race,

That you ran away because you liked being high
And you'd worked on the streets so you could buy
The drugs and stuff—your body craved each day
And all about us—and the life you threw away.

—J. D. Jackson

Inspiration

Drunk drivers. Every death at the hands of a drunk driver is uncalled for. It doesn't matter if it's remembered or not. Innocent people should not be dying because a person chose to drive while drunk. Guilty or not, if you pay a lawyer enough money, he/she will see to it that you stay out of jail. It's time for the lawyers and/or law enforcement personnel to do whatever is necessary to get these individuals off the road and in jail or in prison if necessary.

Faded Memory

I sit here surrounded by these prison walls
Trying to remember things left undone;
And the memories I have keep hounding me,
As I think of that lady and her son.

I remember leaving for work that day
And I can remember going back home.
I remember finding the note on the door
Telling me you were going to be gone.

I know I went out for a drink or two
And I remember talking with friends.
I even remember leaving around midnight,
But then my memory suddenly ends.

Apparently I lost control of the car
And crossed the centerline.
Taking the lives of two innocent people,
Way before their appointed time.

I can't right the wrong I committed that night,
And I can't bring back his wife and son.
But I can honestly beg him and God Almighty
To forgive me for what I've done.

—J. D. Jackson

Inspiration

My son inspired this witty piece. Years ago, he would attempt to make his wife jealous by saying "kitty, kitty" each time he saw a fair damsel. As far as I know, it never worked. So just use your imagination and go with it.

Kitty Kitty

I came home from work
Not expecting a thing;
Ran smack into you and
Made a date for a fling.

If I'm going to step out
And dance the night away,
I'd rather it be with you
To put an end to my day.

As we dance on the floor
And you like what you see,
Just ask me real nice and
I'll take you home with me.

I've got a nice little place—
Enough room, you'll see.
No dogs laying around,
Just room for you and me.

Come here, kitty, kitty,
It's time for us to play.
I've been looking for you
Most of this day.

Come on over, kitty kitty.
You're looking so fine.
And as they come and go,
You're just one of a kind.

−J. D. Jackson

Inspiration

A very determined and confused woman. This marriage is on some very shaky ground. The wife is having some type of crisis in her life and needs a little time to work things out to her own satisfaction. He, on the other hand, has had about enough and is thinking of leaving. However, she's saying to him—If you leave me, take me with you.

Take Me with You

Please take me with you
If you leave home tonight.
I can't make it without you
And I promise not to fight.

I've gotten so used to you
Being here by my side.
And this is not the time
For you to run off and hide.

My words may cut at you
And I'm sorry if I shout.
But I have so many little things
I'm just trying to work out.

So whether you stay here
Or go away if you must.
You're the only real man
Whom I can ever really trust.

I know you're really angry
And I gave you the right.
So take me with you
If you leave home tonight.

But please don't end
Our marriage this way.
I promise to do my part
If you just agree to stay.

—J. D. Jackson

Inspiration

So many people are lost this day and time and, for them, crime is just a way of life. Individuals use and twist religion to satisfy their own beliefs. Nations kill people of a different religion. One day when the truth is known, mountains will fall and every non-believer will be looking for a rock or mountain to hide under. Come back before it's too late. And stay tuned, the best is yet to come.

Come Home To Jesus

Come home to Jesus, little children.
Come back to Him today.
Come home to Jesus, little children.
We'll all kneel down and pray.

Come home to Jesus, little children.
He'll be testing you today.
Come home to Jesus, little children.
Your reward is going to be great.

Come home to Jesus, little children.
His arms are open to us.
Come home to Jesus, little children.
Through faith, hope and trust.

Come home to Jesus, little children.
He's standing there above.
Come home to Jesus, little children.
He'll fill your heart with love.

Come home to Jesus, little children.
Make that decision today.
Come home to Jesus, little children.
We'll all kneel down and pray.

—J. D. Jackson

Inspiration

Please don't get hung up on the sex of the particular individual being referred to; it goes both ways. One person leaves another. It's happening all too often, don't you think? Anyway, the point is this—if you want to leave me, leave me. Don't worry about it. Just go. And what ever you do, don't cry for me.

Dry Your Eyes

Why do you say those things you say to me?
And why all the talk about wanting to be free?
All I ever wanted was to spend my life with you.
What ever happened to the woman I once knew?

You said you were happy when we first met.
But it didn't take long; you just seemed to forget.
And from the beginning you loved me so.
What happened then, I simply don't know.

Life is uncertain and we're tested each day.
It takes love and conviction if both are to stay.
If we ever learn to say no to temptation and lust
We could live our life with the person we trust.

Try as I must, I wasn't able to succeed.
I couldn't find a way to satisfy your needs.
You can't help the way you turned out to be.
And you'll never be happy, until I set you free.

So don't worry about me or where I might go.
There's plenty to do and lots of people I know.
You're not to worry about things you can't see.
Go and dry your eyes and don't cry for me.

Just dry your eyes and don't cry for me.
There's just no stopping what's meant to be.
We gave it a chance; now I'll let you go.
And what happens to me, you'll never know.

—J. D. Jackson

Inspiration

A married couple with some choices to make. The question is this: should we divorce before it even has a chance to succeed or make another attempt to see if it'll work? Think about and use the proper ingredients of a good marriage and it'll stand the test of time. What? Ok— they include the following: God, love, and trust. We've used them for well over thirty-five years and they're guaranteed to work.

One More Chance

We can't seem to help ourselves;
Don't know which way to turn.
But as the years pass slowly by,
The more we tend to learn.

When two people decide to marry,
It's usually based on love.
And some run off together,
While others are blessed from above.

A marriage was meant to last forever
Till death comes one day.
But some tend to forget their vows
And throw it all away.

If God is not part of your life,
You're on the wrong road.
Good marriages begin to improve;
While bad ones tend to erode.

So remember how you got there
And that you're never alone.
Your decision to stay the course
Will help rebuild your home.

So give this marriage one last chance
Before you decide to leave.
If you put aside your differences
There's no need for either to grieve.

Personal Memories and Notes

We work hard and we stumble,
But we seem to find our way.
And in spite of all the hardships
We've both agreed to stay.

Two people so much in love
Can usually work things out.
With the help of God almighty
A marriage is never in doubt.

—J. D. Jackson

Inspiration

As hard as it is for some to believe, things are not always better up north. This person couldn't make it in Boston of all places. Think about it. Well, to make things rhyme, he ended up in Austin. That's in Texas, just in case—never mind. And he did quite well, thank you very much. Now to complete his little world, the love of his life must now join him.

The Gambling Man

I can't make it through tomorrow
If I don't hear from you today.
I'll be filled with so much sorrow
If you don't come out here to stay.

I had to leave you there in Boston;
I couldn't support you on my pay.
I packed my bags for a job in Austin,
And prayed you'd join me one day.

I was determined to save some money,
Just enough to buy us a home.
And even though it's bright and sunny,
I can't stand being here alone.

I've found success and can't turn back
And Austin is where I'll stay.
I pray to God your bags were packed
And you're now well on your way.

I waited patiently for a call to come,
But not one word did I hear.
Arriving home with dinner for one,
I finally had a reason to cheer.

The things we do in the name of love
May never be surpassed.
But thanks to you and God above
This test of love we passed.

—J. D. Jackson

Inspiration

The Lord's Prayer primarily and other prayers I've heard over the years. Is there a right and proper way to pray? I think not. Just talk to God any way you choose. Lying down, standing up, on your knees, on your back, after winning the lottery, or face down in the mud. It just doesn't matter, just as long as you talk to Him. He's waiting.

A Simple Prayer

Father in heaven, I thank you
For everything you've done for me.
I thank you for all of the beauty
That stretches from sea to sea.

Father, I thank you for loving me.
It's so evident by what you've done.
I see it in the glory of the heavens.
I see it in the setting sun.

And, Father, I thank you for the freedom
Used to make my own choices.
I thank you for leading me to a church
That speaks with so many voices.

I ask for the wisdom of Solomon
As I study your book and pray.
And for the faith that Noah had
As you guide me through each day.

I especially need the patience of Job
As he dealt with Satan's wrath.
For patience is vitally important today
If we choose to walk the right path.

Father, I thank you for caring enough
To save me through your Son.
And I thank you for sending Him back
When all your work is done.

Personal Memories and Notes

I pray this day that I am worthy,
And to you I bring no shame.
And I thank you with my heart and soul
And bless your holy name.

                            Amen.

—J. D. Jackson

Inspiration

Two people going in opposite directions. Sometimes romance rules the night. Try romance instead of a fight, and you'll be glad you did. A fight takes you in the wrong direction and usually ends up hurting someone. With romance, though, you always go in the right direction and both individuals usually end up feeling much better about everything.

Talk Softly

Won't you please talk softly to me
And put the love back in your heart?
Just rest your head on my shoulder;
And tell me honestly we'll never part.

You've told me you still love me,
But it's not coming from the heart.
I just don't see the same woman
That I saw from the very start.

You were that one in a million
And you were so filled with love.
I treated you with such kindness,
You had to be blessed from above.

The love we had was so genuine
And I truly loved the romance.
So let's rekindle that love tonight
Before we lose our last chance.

Lay your head on my shoulder
And let all your problems be.
While you think about the good times,
Won't you please talk softly to me.

−J. D. Jackson

Inspiration

A loser.

Satan's Run

The devil is always at work,
And he destroys man and home.
But if you always keep your faith,
You'll never be left alone.

If you stop him at the crossroads,
He'll simply tell you a lie.
If you believe all of his babbling,
Your soul will surely die.

He thought he was so special
With his supernatural condition.
But now he's going to die
For all of his high ambition.

Satan is on the run now,
But he has no place to hide.
Shouldn't that be a lesson for us
Not to have too much pride?

Satan is on the run now.
He's going to loose the final war.
And once the battle is over,
He'll be gone forever more.

—J. D. Jackson

Inspiration

Just a simple childhood friendship. Over time it developed into something much better—Love. Love between two adults. The seed was planted with the first, hello. Time will dictate whether or not it remains a friendship, as some do, or if it has a chance to change. Given the chance, many friendships take on a new ingredient—love.

Friendship

I saw you walking by one day,
And I put my sights on you.
Although I'm nothing to brag about,
I knew what I had to do.

We were just two lonely people
With so many things to learn.
When love decided to come our way,
We couldn't miss our turn?

Yes, I know we grew up together,
And you've always been my friend.
But there's no denying these feelings;
This friendship has got to end.

Time has been a friend of ours;
We're wiser and we've grown.
Deep down I've always loved you.
Being together is better than alone.

So won't you lay here beside me,
And just let me hold you tight?
I promise I'll always love you,
Won't you stay with me tonight?

—J. D. Jackson

Inspiration

A simple ride in the country. Remember this-you don't have to live in the country to enjoy the country. My aunt and uncle were from Utica, NY, and they showed me this many years ago. At times, I would visit them during the summer and while there; we took a number of trips to the country. They just wanted to enjoy the peace and solitude a drive in the country offered them.

A Ride in the Country

Let's take a ride in the country,
If only to look around.
It sure beats riding the streets
Of any old city or town.

If you take a ride in the country,
You'll always get to see
Just a little piece of heaven
In this, the land of the free.

When you go for a ride in the country,
You can take a horse or a car.
And compared to city driving,
Out here, you can really go far.

When you go for a ride in the country,
Your anxieties are always less.
But if you take a ride in the city
You increase your level of stress.

So come visit us here in the country.
When you really feel the need.
You might consider a car or truck,
Or even a four-legged steed.

Come on out here to the country,
If you're really feeling down.
Just make up your mind and do it,
And leave that busy little town.

—J. D. Jackson

Inspiration

Not to be confused with the infamous Trail of Tears we associate with the movement of the Cherokee Indian tribe. This is just another love between a man and a woman problem. It's a lost love; I still care about you, come and find me type problem. Exactly—it's another spin on love.

Trail of Tears

I cry and cry myself to sleep
When you're not around to see.
I'm so afraid to be alone;
I wish you were here with me.

The thing I cherish above all else
Is having you by my side.
But life on earth is never that easy
For people with too much pride.

How'd I let myself get trapped
By a man such as you?
I was so content just being alone,
Until a dream of mind came true.

But dreams are quickly shattered
When love changes our plan.
And love will lead to happiness
If you ever find the right man.

Won't you come looking for me again
And take away all my fears?
I've made it so easy for you this time—
Just follow my trail of tears.

−J. D. Jackson

Inspiration

Spending a lot of hot summer afternoons at the movies watching the latest western. How can we ever forget the cowboy? Although it originated in colonial times, the word cowboy is now associated with Roy Rogers, Gene Autry, Lash LaRue, Bob Steele, and many others. Let's keep the memory alive.

Cowboys

Who's going to be the next cowboy?
Who's going to sing the next song?
Gene and Roy have passed away
And gone to their final home.

Who's going to be the next cowgirl
That will ride and sing along?
Dale and Annie have passed away
And gone to their final home.

Don't ever forget what they taught us
On those long, hot summer days—
That good always triumphs over evil—
Before we were set in our ways.

Will there ever be another cowboy
Who can ride and sing a song,
And round up all of the bad guys
To send to their final home?

Are you going to be the next cowboy?
Can you sing and carry a song?
Are you destined to join the others
When you go to your final home?

When was the west finally won,
And where have the cowboys gone?
Will we ever see another one
Ride off into the sunset alone?

—J. D. Jackson

Inspiration

The over-the-road driver has a difficult, lonely and somewhat under-appreciated job. If he's married, it's even worse. Just remember that loyalty goes both ways. Important reminder: keep your butt in the truck. Think about it.

Long Haul Driver

I came back early from a run out to Boise
And decided to surprise my wife.
I finished my log and got home around midnight
And received the surprise of my life.

The woman I married played me for a fool
And decided to go out on me.
While riding the roads just delivering my loads,
She did every man she could see.

If wives are to wait patiently back home,
They expect the same out of you.
Each time you decide to stop at a bar,
Just imagine what she's up to.

You both work hard and have a job to do.
Suspicions you don't need anymore.
If you're on the road and she's back home,
Just keep the lizards away from your door.

The long haul driver needs to have a woman
Who will never take him for a ride.
It's you she loves and not a job you chose
And should always stand by your side.

—J. D. Jackson

Inspiration

The Want Ads. Job-hunting. That's it. Simple, yes? Some people have a job that will last a lifetime, while others continually shop around. Chances are everyone reading this has read through the classifieds for one reason or another.

The Want Ads

While scanning the want ads, it caught my eye.
Some exciting jobs were open at the FBI.
I couldn't see passing up on something like this,
Even knowing full well there was a lot I would miss.

Positions such as these require keen observation,
A gift for the gab and lots of self-determination.
It helps to have nerves when you back down a stare.
And use your senses, never take a dare.

With a position such as this, learn what you must.
Before you go to the field, you'll earn some trust.
Some long term planning would be a necessary tool
For those with ambitions or getting out of school.

You can advance up the ladder if you wait your turn.
So hone the skills you have and find others to learn.
Neither age nor gender should ever get in your way.
This field is open if you're strong enough to stay.

Know what you're talking about then get it in gear.
If you know what to do, you eliminate the fear.
Always mean what you say and say what you mean.
Be fair and consistent and keep your record clean.

When the time comes, there should never be doubt.
If there's ever any question, just pull your record out.
Those in your way will play games with your mind.
If someone moves ahead, another stay's behind.

—J. D. Jackson

Inspiration

Traveling and getting lost. Believe you me, I got lost many times. On one occasion, I even pulled a Chevy Chase and got us lost in East St. Louis, IL. Just like a man, isn't it? Anyway, this one has a little twist to it. Instead of driving down a road and getting lost, these two are driving down one of life's highways and are getting lost. Different roads, same results.

We've Been Down This Road Before

Sweetheart, you have always been the apple of my eye.
And no, I was never happy to see you sad or cry.
But it seems like every time I tried to make things right,
Somehow I'd find a way to end it with a fight.

No, I never really wanted things to end up this way,
And I could never find the words to make you stay.
You've seen right through me from the very start.
And I knew all along, you were bright and smart.

So go now, you've obviously given this much thought.
And to ask you to stay again would just be for naught.
You're right, neither of us knows what life has in store.
And yes, I do agree. We've been down this road before.

You remember how good things were from the start?
I did those silly things just to try and win your heart.
Yes, I know we had some special times back then,
And I wonder if I'll ever get to see or touch you again.

No, I never realized I was putting your needs last.
I'm so sorry for the pain I caused you in the past.
With much regret, I'll have to let you go this time.
But on this occasion, the pain and suffering are mine.

So go now, you've obviously given this much thought.
And to ask you to stay again would just be for naught.
You're right, neither of us knows what life has in store.
And yes, I do agree. We've been down this road before.

—J. D. Jackson

Inspiration

A man has done everything he thought a lady wanted done. Her response to him was—what about love? Goes to show you doesn't it, money really can't buy everything? So make sure you say from time to time, I love you, I love you, I love you.

What About Love?

The longer we're together, the more I know you care.
Our love got its start when I caught you in a stare.
We have a lot in common and how I hate to waste.
Let's not destroy our love by our selfish use of haste.

People have waited a lifetime to find the right mate.
Others may lose out because they wait too late.
You and I were lucky to find each other this soon.
And I truly love our walks under a full-lit moon.

Our relationship has flourished and has room to grow.
But if it's to last, we must take it nice and slow.
Let's fight these desires even if it ends in bliss.
And like days of old, let's end this night with a kiss.

I've seen many sides of you since we first met.
And I appreciate the things you've given me; yet
I've waited months for words inspired from above.
Think for a moment, have you ever said the word—love?

    I do enjoy our time together.
    I love that penthouse above.
    I even enjoy the talks we have
    But what about love?

—J. D. Jackson

Inspiration

The fairy tale. None in particular, just a simple spoof on the ever popular fairy tale theme. But one attempt after another to come up with an idea eventually took me in this direction. Well, maybe next time. I hope the kids will enjoy the ending anyway.

The Last Fairy Tale

I tried to think of a new fairy tale
To read to the kids at night.
But everything that came to mind
Would simply give them a fright.

I was standing in my kitchen one day
Just looking for something to use.
I thought about the pie and the egg,
But no words came forth to amuse.

I thought of sitting a kid in a corner
But that had already been done.
And then I saw an itsy bitsy spider,
But there could never be but one.

I knew it would have to be original
Something witty to make a kid smile.
But every time I put pen to paper,
It would end up in a large pile.

So I decided to end this project
As I could think of nothing new.
That being the case, it's never too late
To say, "Good night-I Love you."

—J. D. Jackson

Inspiration

Churches we've attended over the years. As you look around yours, you'll probably see the elderly, the women and children, and a dash of young teens. But for the most part, where have the men gone?

Where Have All the Men Gone?

We go to church and we sit around.
We listen to the choir sing.
Deacon gets up and reads some words,
And we hear the bells ring.

Preacher steps forward, pulls out his notes
And talks about the man on the throne.
We listen closely as we look around
And wonder: Where have all the men gone?

It's November, the deer begin to run,
And the man is preaching about sin.
Then comes February, the race is starting
And we're wondering, who's going to win?

The very next time you go to church,
Take a quick look around.
Our seniors, women and children are there,
But the men are nowhere to be found.

Other activities aren't such a bad thing
When taken as a whole,
But the man upstairs would truly like to be
The winner of your eternal soul.

So go to church next Sunday, men,
And be with family and friends.
Things you do in the name of God
Will always help you in the end.

—J. D. Jackson

Inspiration

A little twist concerning the black sheep of the family. This time however, it's the aunt and not the uncle or brother. Disclaimer: most of us have aunts, and for the most part, they are good and beautiful people. This is a ha-ha type thing, so don't take it seriously—chill.

Aunt Bertha

Have you ever had an aunt Bertha?
One that kept her house so-so.
And every time you went for a visit,
She was always telling you, no no.

Did you ever feel bad just being there,
Especially if someone was smoking?
Did she ever go around wiping up ashes
Or act like she may have been choking?

Did she always think she was a good one
And always talk nice around you?
And as soon as you left her magnificence,
She'd give her house a good walk-through.

Can you ever remember a kind word,
Or a day when she wasn't mean?
I bet you'll never forget this woman
Who could fuss, drink, and clean.

If you think this was written about you,
Just think of what makes it so.
Learn to laugh, smile, and enjoy life
And think of a new way to go.

—J. D. Jackson

Inspiration

The original citizens of this country. Those now called the American Indian. To my knowledge, no race of people has ever been used and abused like our native citizens. Although we're not responsible for the action or deeds of our forefathers, we as a free people can at least acknowledge it.

The Native American

If the time ever came to make things right,
What would we do with this land?
When our forefathers came over here,
You know it was in another's hand.

Columbus thought he was in the Indies,
And gave these people a name.
And over the centuries since that time,
The name Indian has remained the same.

Some viewed them as a prime example
Of man in his natural state;
But left to the whims of the settlers,
They would have surely met their fate.

The time has come to honor them
And to some that made them proud.
When John Smith needed real help,
The princess Pocahontas spoke loud.

Surely you've heard the name Geronimo
Used when you jump from a great height.
It took the army three years to catch him.
Great Chieftains just know how to fight.

Words of Inspiration

Surely He shall deliver thee from the snare of
the fowler,
And from the noisome pestilence.
He shall cover thee with His feathers,
And under His wings shalt thou trust:
His truth shall be thy shield and buckler.

Psalms 91:3-4

Do you know the story of chief Sitting Bull
Or at least of Custer's last stand?
He thought he could defeat the Sioux chief,
But Custer was to loose every last man.

We can't leave out Chief Crazy Horse,
An Indian who refused to give in;
Or the Indian known as Jim Thorpe,
The greatest athlete the world had seen.

The unwritten language of the Navaho
Was important in so many ways.
It helped us defeat our enemies,
And gave us peace for all these days.

Relics of their day were cast in stone,
And many have gone away;
But on the monument of Iwo Jima,
You'll find the Indian—Ira Hayes.

It would surely take volumes of books
To name and to recognize
Each one for their contributions,
Who have walked beneath the skies.

—J. D. Jackson

Inspiration

Teachers, those of this country and all throughout the world. Teachers are important to all of us, and just like other professions, some of them are better than others. For the most part they're getting the job done. I can still remember some of mine, even after all these many years. That includes you, Ms. Inscoe. Well, how about you? Which one made a mark on your life?

The Teacher

It's so hard to get through life
On your very own,
And not all have had someone
To help them along.

Little children depend on us
Just to make it through.
As you think back over time,
Who was there for you?

Many children are watched over
By their mom and dad.
While others had to make do
On something they never had.

More and more depend on others
For all their daily care.
If called upon in times of need,
Grandma was always there.

Who helped you make it through
The days of thick and thin?
Maybe showed you the way,
Or even wiped your chin?

Who was it that introduced you
To the wondrous things there?
Did you ever see them bite a lip
Or even pull their hair?

Personal Memories and Notes

Over the years they witnessed
So many of us come and go.
And being with us every day,
It was hard to see us grow.

Many had a hand in directing
What we were to do.
So to all of the teachers past and present
—Thank you.

–J. D. Jackson

Inspiration

This was just another silly attempt at a good laugh. As my grandson would say, "You get, you get it?" Well, anyway. Misdirect them, then bring 'em home.

Silver Tongued Devil

Talk about the man that's-on the prowl.
You know he never stops till he-gets the gal.
The words keep coming till she-gives in.
One is going to lose and-he'll win.

The ladies go out on a-Friday night.
Guys look around till-one's in sight.
When a lock is made on-one of them.
All they do next is-reel them in.

Once they're both sitting in-one place.
Only thing left is to-start the race.
Man moves first with a-"Hi there."
Lady is next with a-seductive stare.

It's a tie up to this point-of the game.
Lady asks quickly-"What's your name?"
Caught off guard he says-"John Smith."
Well, tell me now, John-"Who you with?"

Came by myself now-don't you know?
Any place in town you'd-like to go?
Well, I do have a place that's-on my mind.
Then he says to himself its a-good sign.

You silver-tongued devil, where you-taking me?
It's a special little place that's-built for three.
And nothing's going to happen till-we're alone.
There's no need to worry cause-we're at home.

Personal Memories and Notes

Poetic Justice

Well, I enjoyed our night out-on the town.
Junior's in bed so-what now?
Let me think for a minute and-we'll see.
Go grab a sandwich and I'll-get the TV.

—J. D. Jackson

Inspiration

I've always known there was a better way to spend a weekend. From time to time, I've overheard people say they were going out to buy a bottle and get drunk. Why? Why would any person want to get drunk just for the sake of getting drunk? From what are they trying to escape? They and the Lord know. My way is better, and I'll practically guarantee that you will not have a hangover on any given Monday morning.

A Weekend High

Weekends by far are the best days of the week,
Especially since meeting you.
Why couldn't there be more days like these?
Why give us just the two?

I've never had such a time filled with joy,
Never these sights to see.
And there's never been such a time in my life,
I was this happy and carefree.

From the depths of despair to just feeling good,
I owe so much to you.
Simply being with you so intoxicates my mind,
I need time just to renew.

You've taken me to heights I've never seen before,
So I'll tell you by and by.
The rest of the week will provide me the time
To come down from a weekend high.

You've enlightened my mind to many new things.
You gave meaning to my life.
You made each day better than the last.
Won't you please be my wife?

−J. D. Jackson

Inspiration

Politicians, what else? Those who spend the people's money on a hole dug just because the dirt was there. Those who give away our natural resources and, we the people, get practically nothing in return. Those who will build a dam on a dry river bed just to get the people's money into the hands of their friends. Those who spend the people's money on worthless projects simply because a lobbyist gave them or their campaign some money. Those who refuse to let a good bill proceed until they ruin it with their own worthless amendment, etc, etc. Just remember that, we the people own this country and we put you in office. So do what is right and good for the country, not your friends.

A Politician's Life

The politician's life can be a lonely life
If they leave their spouse back home.
Once the sessions and meetings are done,
They must spend their time alone.

The nation's capital can be a cruel place
To those not wise to the ways.
It'll eat you up and spit you out,
Make you wish at home you'd stayed.

Dare I say that some have found a way
To get around the lonely nights?
Those who've been there a term or two
Have apparently learned how to fight.

And money being the root of all evil
Can easily lead one into sin.
And once you start selling our trust
Other forms of evil creep in.

Does Mr. Smith still work in Washington?
Do the lobbyists still work the halls?
Do greed and corruption still rule the day?
And is our nation headed for a fall?

We the people always sit and wonder
How our officials lose their sight.
What's so difficult about going to work
And doing what you know is right?

–J. D. Jackson

Inspiration

A fellow at work who is always cutting down that which he does not understand. The United States Coast Guard is the best-kept secret of our uniformed services. God bless all current and past members, enlisted and officer alike.

The Forgotten Military

There's an uniformed service of America
That usually doesn't come to one's mind.
It's small if you're talking about numbers,
But so grand, it's just one of a kind.

They don't parade for the Unknown Soldier,
Nor stand at our embassy doors.
But you can find them at various locations;
You can find them on America's shores.

They have nothing like the Blue Angels,
Nor do they fly like the great Thunderbirds.
They serve proudly and protect our nation
Much better than you've probably heard.

Even though they're ignored by many,
Yet called upon in times of great need.
They're trained and ready to respond
And can assist you with record speed.

Any time you head out on the ocean,
And the conditions are getting hard;
Or a flood is surrounding your family,
Call on the United States Coast Guard.

—J. D. Jackson

Inspiration

I'd like to say that one of God's greatest creations-the female-inspired this particular piece, but that's not the case. It was written after observing inmates at the bathroom mirror. Speaking of the male inmate only. They were observed at the mirror for up to two hours or more. They brush, they pluck, they blow, they comb, they wash, then they re-wash, they look, then they step closer to the mirror and look some more. They turn left, they turn right, and then they get someone to look at the back of their head. They floss, they gargle, they spit, they check each hair, they shave, and they walk away for a few moments and then return to the same spot and repeat things already done. I could go on and on—ladies; you don't even come close.

Vanity

Vanity is not such a bad thing.
No, that's not always the case.
Some women are naturally beautiful
No need for stuff on your face

And it's usually associated with beauty,
But even that's not always true.
What's wrong with paint and polish,
If it makes you feel better about you?

Now the time we waste on vanity
Could be put to better use.
But when compared to other vices,
Is there really that much abuse?

I can't see a real problem with vanity,
Especially for someone like me.
The time spent in front of my mirror
Creates this beauty for you to see.

Think of the time we waste on vanity
And the cost to fix hair and face,
Only to have the wind and the rain
Destroy all that beauty and grace.

You say you don't have to listen,
Even though the talk is true.
Vanity is really not a good thing
For beautiful people like you.

–J. D. Jackson

Inspiration

The rape and murder of our children and grandchildren. I sometimes wonder what I would do in a certain situation involving one of my own. The judicial system has no idea what to do about these people—those who rape, kill, or molest our women, and especially the children. So much money is being wasted on them, and what are we getting in return? But then, we have to maintain hope. Hope that some of the counseling and therapy will do some good. Hope that they will not repeat the crime that got them sent to prison. As for their punishment, maybe we should ask the victims, get a general consensus from each and respond accordingly.

What Life Form Are You?

There are so many different life forms
Walking the earth today.
It's so easy to see what you look like
And I hear the things you say.

Yes, I know we were given dominion
Over various forms of life.
They reduce our labor, feed or comfort us
Or provide some parts for a knife.

I suppose it's because of our brain size,
Which lets us think things out.
Or could it be the use of two legs
That allows man to move about.

Well, if man is all that intelligent,
Why can't he just stop and think?
What drives him to beat a woman
Until her eyes no longer blink?

What makes people young and old
Act out the way they do?
How can a human perform sexual acts
On a child the age of two?

These are ugly and despicable things
Some humans tend to do.
And the question I'd like to ask is-
What life form are you?

—J. D. Jackson

Inspiration

A long and enjoyable life with the woman you married. No divorce. Handle the calm waters just as you would the stormy waters. Do the best you can with all your days and don't forget to dream a bit. The life these two had together is passing through her mind as the preacher is giving the eulogy.

My Last Good-bye

When was the last time I said good-bye to him?
As I sit quietly on this bench, I can't remember when.
I know we were together for, oh, so many years.
The Lord knows that over time I shed a million tears.

We fell so madly in love at such a young and tender age.
Preacher said, "Is this what you want?" as he turned the page.
We didn't even have the money for a proper honeymoon,
But he said, "Don't worry honey, we'll be going real soon."

The military took him away from me one cold October day.
And he liked the life so very much, he simply decided to stay.
We moved and traveled around for about twenty years or so.
Then we gave it all up one day with no particular place to go.

We finally stayed put for awhile somewhere around the coast,
But ended up moving one last time to where jobs were the most.
Crazy man would try everything that seemed to come along.
One day he tried his very best to write a country song.

As I think back, I really enjoyed the times we had together.
He was funny, serious, a real pain, but out of line, never.
And I guess if he could ask me again, I'd just have to say yes.
The eulogy ended, the preacher said, "Ma'am, its time, I guess."

As our family and friends gathered around the gravesite,
They kept asking if I was going to be all right.
As the preacher said the final words with eyes looking high,
I placed my rose, threw him kiss and said my last good-bye.

—J. D. Jackson

Inspiration

The youngsters who are called away to fight our wars. Since the world can't find a way to live in peace, a standing army is a necessary thing. Unfortunately, some of the men ordered to defend our country never return. As for me, I'd rather die defending this country and what it stands for, instead of running away like so many have done in the past.

Carry Me Home

Please carry me home
When my days are through.
And bury me there
So I'll be close to you.

You know the place
Where I want to be.
Over by the clearing
Under that sycamore tree.

You think on it for awhile
The memory will come back.
It's the last thing you heard
As bags were being packed.

We've finished our training
And will be put to the test.
But before we ship out
We're just getting some rest.

When we finish our mission
And the news leaks out.
You may cry some tears
Or will jump and shout.

In the weeks that will come,
If you don't hear from me.
When you read these words,
You'll begin to see.

—J. D. Jackson

Inspiration

Jesus hanging on the cross. His purpose for being sent here to earth. His last words as his job was now finished.

It Is Finished

Consider the pain of a crown of thorns
And the blood trickling down your face.
Think of the burden of dragging a cross,
Especially at such a slow pace.

What's there to say, as you stand there alone,
Listening to the judge's commands?
Can you imagine the pain of having the nails
Pierce your feet and your hands?

Was He thinking about us or things to be,
As they laughed, gambled and jeered?
And was He still conscious and alive as
The centurion pierced Him with a spear?

Why would He suffer the shame and torment
For people like you and me?
If the day ever came for us to choose,
Would we stand up for Him to see?

Imagine the thoughts going through His mind,
As His precious life diminished?
And what did He know as He hung on the cross
And said the words; "It is finished?"

Jesus gave up everything for us
Sacrificing His life and limb.
The least we as a people can do,
Is to thank God for sending us Him.

—J. D. Jackson

Inspiration

This piece was written about neighbors in general and is meant to be comical. It's only fictional. We're very fortunate to have neighbors that actually speak to each other. With society being the way it is today, we're fortunate indeed.

The Neighbors

As neighbors come and go,
It seems ours puts us to the test.
They borrow everything we've got
And never give us any rest.

Many have built front porches,
And we put ours on the back.
You'd think that would be okay,
But they never give us any slack.

Why couldn't their kids be like ours
And stay in their own yard?
Why are they allowed to run around
And make our lives so hard?

Their only dog is so unfriendly
And barks real loud if you hit it.
And every time he comes to visit
He will always leave a deposit.

We've always tried to be neighborly;
We always wave and say, "Hey."
But no one ever comes for a visit,
Not even on a special day.

What gets into people these days
That causes them to raise such a fuss?
If you learn to mind your own business,
You could be perfect people like us.

−J. D. Jackson

Inspiration

This piece concerns those of us who have a comfortable life. A good job, family, and a home. But then something snaps, and a few of us throw it all away by turning to other women, men, drugs or alcohol. How sad.

What Is — What Was

When the lights go out on the party.
And there's no more praises to sing,
You take a look back over the years:
Can't seem to remember a thing.

Could it be this drink I hold in my hand,
Or this gray hair on my head?
What is it that causes people to slip
And sometimes wish they were dead?

I had a wife, a family and home,
But gave up and threw it away.
Kept drinking the booze and fooling around:
Will regret it till the end of my day.

I walk the streets both day and night,
Just staying around my kind.
I beg and scrounge for things to sell
To buy my next bottle of wine.

Why can't we learn to accept the things
Our God gave you and me?
Why do we keep looking around
For the things not meant to be?

—J. D. Jackson

Inspiration

With the decline of union representation nationwide, corporations are taking everything they can from the workers of our country. What's happening is that we get lower paying jobs with longer working hours, and benefits which are being slashed to the bone. Workers have always done their share and are willing to make needed sacrifices. But with soaring profits and the astronomical salaries and other perks for the good and bad CEO's of big corporations, etc, don't tell us the money is **not** there.

A Forty-Hour Week

Give me a forty-hour week
With my forty-hour pay.
I'll work real hard for you
The rest of my day.

These twelve-hour jobs
Are definitely not for me.
If you give me a choice,
I'll go with family.

What good does it do us
To work all the time?
If we're not driving a truck,
We're on an assembly line.

Tell me what they've done
With the forty-hour week.
And tell me why they leave
Every time we want to speak.

Working hard for a living
Is an important part of life.
But what good is the money,
If we end up losing our wife?

–J. D. Jackson

Inspiration

First, there was the vast open range of the west. Then came the barbed wire and, finally, the fences. The open range was no more. Today we have homes and entire neighborhoods that are fenced in. What's next?

The Open Range

Why did they have to fence the prairie in?
Why couldn't we all run free?
A man and his horse have to roam about,
With no constraints for him and me.

And how can we move the cattle up north
With all these fence lines in the way?
Why does our way of life have to end?
Is the railroad here to stay?

Remember the days when the west was young,
And everything was ours to take?
But the line of people never seemed to stop.
They all seemed to have a stake.

They came in droves with families in tow,
Just looking for a place to settle down.
The land was so vast, many found a place
Without a neighbor anywhere around.

Why can't the west just stay the way it is?
Why does it have to change?
The west we knew will never be the same,
Because there's no more open range.

—J. D. Jackson

Inspiration

A simple look at life and what it would take to make one man happy.

A Cherry Pie

I know the kind of woman you say you are.
You've told me time and again.
But at the moment I'm not looking around;
I'd just like to call you my friend.

I know you can care for a house just right,
And you say you will tend to my yard.
What bothers me most at this point in time
Is, why are you trying so hard?

I've been here alone for all these years,
And I'm not ready to settle down.
I can't figure out what it is you see
And why things have to be now.

Lord knows I grow weaker by the day.
You're a sight for my poor eyes.
Yes, there's one sure way to win my heart-
Just bake me a good cherry pie.

The woman who bakes me a good cherry pie
Should make a very good wife.
To the woman who bakes the best cherry pie,
I'll dedicate the rest of my life.

It doesn't take much to make me happy
And that should be plain to see.
So if you'll just agree to do your part
You can leave the rest up to me.

—J. D. Jackson

Inspiration

The first lady, Laura Bush and all of the individuals who chose to be a librarian.

The Librarian

She sits at her desk most of the day,
Just looking so proper and trim.
Her hair pulled back, walking shoes on,
With no time to think about men.

A life dedicated to the written word,
Totally consumed by all of her work.
When you walk in and make the noise,
She'll look up and give you a smirk.

Is it the romance, intrigue or boredom,
That works on some people this way?
What else could cause such a person
To become a librarian these days?

It's such a fine and noble profession,
Intended for only a few.
And in order to protect our treasures,
Only the best will ever do.

−J. D. Jackson

Inspiration

To all of the sisters of this world, and especially the sister
my wife never had. While growing up, a brother or sister
can be a friend or a big pain in the rear. But later in life,
you will turn to them in your times of need. When your
parents eventually pass on, you will have blood to help you
grieve. Being an only child may be good for the parents,
but I venture to say that the child will regret it time and
time.

Sisters

She has always been there
Through thick and through thin,
I'm pleased and oh, so honored
To call her my friend.

I know there were times
When we couldn't get along;
But, thank our lucky stars,
We had a good home.

Over time I was able to see
The woman she was to be,
By the way she treated others
And took care of me.

There were things she did
That nobody else would try.
During my times of sorrow
She'd even dry my eyes.

A cancer robbed me of my
Best friend this day.
And God sent an angel
To take my sister away.

Why'd she get sick and
Why'd she have to leave?
I miss her so very much,
And to this day I grieve.

—J. D. Jackson

Inspiration

How many times have you been urged to do a certain job
or task around the house? But somehow you knew that it
wasn't the right day for that particular job. Today is for
fishing, golf, football or rest. Mowing the grass or the
other choirs can wait for that particular kind of day.

A Particular Kind Of Day

I'm sometimes asked why I don't cut the grass,
Or at least clean up the yard.
There are times in a day when a man has to play
And try not to work so hard.

I came home from work, entered the house,
And took a quick look around.
I wondered out loud why things were a mess,
She said she just had to lie down.

Every one knows there are certain days
Not suitable for this or that.
As soon as you're ready to cut the grass,
Your son wants to go swing a bat.

Today you planned to clean the bedroom
Down at the end of the hall.
But girlfriend one came up with a plan
For two to go shopping at the mall.

It should be clear to you by now
It's not laziness that you see.
Even though we have different agendas
We're the same you and me.

There's so much to do around this house,
And I hear all the words you say.
And of all people, you should know by now,
We must wait for a particular kind of day.

—J. D. Jackson

Inspiration

The high school seniors looking back over their time in school. Remembering the good times and the bad. Some begin to look to the future while others know they have none. But for this brief period of time, they're equals. Each one of them has accomplished the same goal. They have finally graduated. Some friendships will now end as they go there separate ways, and others will continue for awhile. A very few will last a lifetime.

The Last Twelve Years

One of life's little milestones
Every parent gets to enjoy,
Concerns our sweet little children,
Every single girl and boy.

It occurs near the age of six,
If you give or take a year.
Though moms and dads may love it,
The children leave home in fear.

But once they finally settle down and
Begin their first day of school,
They learn to have a real good time.
They may learn the golden rule.

Little do they realize that
Over the next twelve years,
There'll be many days of laughter,
And they'll shed a million tears.

But as they grow into adulthood
And maybe choose a career,
They'll soon forget their troubles
And dwell on the last twelve years.

—J. D. Jackson

Inspiration

At this particular point in my life, I'm still not convinced that every human being has a conscience. But I do believe that there comes a time in our lives when we must weigh the benefits of a life of crime, as compared to a so-called normal life. The jails and prisons hold only a small percentage of the ones who chose the wrong path. The rest are still on the streets and they have an unlimited source of victims, us.

A *Life of Crime*

Does it really matter to anyone
If your skin is black or white?
Good and evil can't know color.
Both think they're always right.

Some follow in the steps of a hero
And do some good with their lives,
While others choose the wrong path
And end up with guns and knives.

If left totally up to the good side,
All evil would pay some price.
If the evil side is given a chance,
They will gladly take your life.

What do you think causes people
To end up going the wrong way?
Do we always do the right thing
By helping them the rest of our day?

When a preacher saves a living soul,
He's usually a very happy man.
If we can turn one life from crime,
We know we've done all we can.

Every last crime big or small
Will be judged by God one day.
But it's up to man to do the right thing
And take the murderers life away.

−J. D. Jackson

Inspiration

The lifesavers of this world. Those who risk their own lives to possibly save another. Is there a better gift to give someone than a second chance at life? I think not.

The Rescue

We live and we struggle
To make something of our time.
But many will pass away
Without something to call mine.

But, as for me I'm satisfied,
And I can proudly say
Some people were allowed to live
At least for one more day.

I've rescued from death's door
Children, a father, or brother.
How can I decide if either one
Was worth more than another?

Not one of them was old enough
Or able to say at the time,
But as I think back over the years
Thank you never entered my mind.

I was happy in just knowing
That I'd done my very best.
They were back in the hands of God,
And He would take care of the rest.

—J. D. Jackson

Inspiration

Just one imaginary young man from the old west. A snapshot of a life that could have been.

The Shooter

Down in the hills of Kentucky,
A young lad hones his skills.
He learns how to handle a gun,
And he learns what it means to kill.

He was guided by the hands of his dad,
As he learned to live off the land.
And as he continued to improve his skills,
He grew quicker with the use of his hand.

He was always looking for adventure
And decided he had to leave now.
After hearing stories from a drifter,
He headed toward El Paso town.

He arrived on a hot summer day
And decided to go for a drink.
Trouble followed him through the door,
And he shot before he had time to think.

From that day forward, it hounded him,
As his reputation seemed to grow.
He hit everything his eye could see,
And he was tested everywhere he'd go.

The shooter never stayed in one place.
He was always moving around.
He knew if he ever dropped his guard,
His home would be in the ground.

Personal Memories and Notes

And as he traveled from place to place,
His age finally slowed him down.
One day he decided to hang up the gun,
And get lost in an East Coast town.

—J. D. Jackson

Inspiration

The times that we have been denied advances or promotions because of the games some people insist on playing.

The Games People Play

Have you ever jumped off a building
Pretending that you could fly,
Then realizing a few moments later
On the ground you did lie?

And do you remember having a party
With all your little friends?
You served them coffee and cookies,
Until your mother called you in.

Then, on your last business trip,
Did you decide to enter a bar?
As you removed your wedding ring,
Did you tell her who you really are?

You left the house early today
To visit your very best friend.
While you sat there and reminisced,
Was she aware you'd done her in?

Games people play can be so enjoyable
Or pierce you like the tip of a knife.
Wouldn't we be a lot better off,
If deception wasn't a part of our life?

—J. D. Jackson

Inspiration

The amazing story of a slave ship captain and the beauty he left the world.

The Sea Captain

Amazing Grace was written one day
As the preacher sat at his desk.
He'd crossed the Atlantic on a sailing ship
And was beginning to feel the unrest.

The life of a captain is a lonely one,
With nobody to call a friend.
Destined to spend their nights alone,
They were captains to the very end.

He would leave England time and again
To sail for the African coast.
There he traded for a human cargo
And always demanded the most.

Growing so tired of seeing the misery,
He anchored in his very last slip.
John Newton was this man's name,
And he was the captain of a slave ship.

One day he became a preacher of God,
Giving up his wretched past.
And ended up writing hundreds of hymns,
Which gave meaning to his life at last.

For Amazing Grace was written one day
By a wretch such as he.
Our God worked in a mysterious way
And took John Newton off the sea.

—J. D. Jackson

Inspiration

A term used often in some of the early westerns shown regularly during the fifties and sixties. Slang for anybody not from the country.

The City Slicker

For most of the people raised in the city,
There's no other life they'd have.
Some know the back streets and alleys
Like we know the trails and paths.

When they want to see nature at its best,
They'll find a ride to the zoo.
And when they have a desire for fish,
The corner market will always do.

In the heat of summer, if they want to swim,
They go to the neighborhood pool.
In order to see the planets and stars,
A planetarium is really cool.

If the smell of the city is in their blood
And the sights and sounds are great,
The life and pace of people in the country
Is a life they can't tolerate.

Our lives are in perfect harmony
When referring to where we live.
But if we had to give up one for the other,
The city would have to give.

−J. D. Jackson

Inspiration

The decade of the sixties and the way it changed the world.

A Child of the Sixties

We're a child of the sixties,
But we did all right.
Some turned to drugs while
Others went to fight.

If we knew everything about
The drugs and more,
They probably killed as many
As the Vietnam War.

The war and drugs were the
Craze back then.
The war on either we could
Never win.

There was too much money from
The drugs and booze,
With politicians in charge we
Were destined to lose.

Summers were a time for the
Song and dance.
You're always better off making
Love and romance.

Words of Inspiration

Excellent speech becometh not a fool:
Much less do lying lips a prince.
                              Proverbs 17:7

Why did so many choose
A political fight?
When nothing they ever did
Made the world just right.

No way of knowing how many
Stayed, as they should.
But for those who went to fight,
They did what they could.

If you chose to run away,
You'll always have doubt
What fighting for your country
Is really about.

But as the years passed us by,
We found our place.
Many are wearing business suits.
A few chose lace.

There's not a day I would trade
If ever I needed.
The things we've experienced
Will never be repeated.

–J. D. Jackson

Inspiration

The simple question which is—What do you have?

What Do You Have?

What do you have when there's no more pain?
What do you have when there's no more rain?
What do you have when there's no more sorrow?
You have the beginnings of a new tomorrow.

What's going to happen when there's no more hate?
The world begins to change and it's never too late.
And how would we feel if we never cried again?
One day we'll know when He eliminates the sin.

For sin is the cause of our troubles today,
And when He returns, it'll be taken away.
It's been a few years since He went back home,
And, just as He promised, we've never been alone.

How would it feel to have no more dying?
We'll know one day and there'll be no denying.
He's returned to us, as He promised He would,
And will read out the list of those who were good.

That's the day we've been working toward.
And for all who refused, He'll settle the score.
When all former things have passed away,
We'll live with Him for the rest of our days.

—J. D. Jackson

Inspiration

The twisted outlook some people have concerning beauty or how to look good. The young people who starve themselves to death because they think they look better.

Wafer Thin

Can you remember the day
Of the blond bombshell?
We had Marilyn Monroe
And Jane Mansfield.

These ladies were smart
And they had looks to beat;
But when they sat at the table,
They had plenty to eat.

What's all the fuss about
Being wafer thin?
Sit down for a bite,
Like they did back then.

But think of moderation
When it comes to eating.
With too much or too little,
A doctor you'll be meeting.

Be the kind of person
You really want to be.
And put meat on your bones
For the people to see.

−J. D. Jackson

Inspiration

Since parents no longer arrange marriages, it takes a chance meeting between two consenting adults before a relationship can truly develop.

Chance Meeting

Won't you sit a spell
And lighten your load?
Let's have some coffee
Before we hit the road.

I saw you last night as
I was having my meal,
Wanted to talk while
You were making a deal.

I've been coming here
For just a little while,
But never seen a woman
With such a pretty smile.

I would really like to
Know you a little better.
Give me your address and
I'll write you a letter.

Yes, I know it's not done
Very much anymore.
But I can still remember
Getting mail by the door.

Before I come back
I'll drop you a line.
And if you'll agree to it
We'll meet for a time.

—J. D. Jackson

Inspiration

Discussions I've had over the years with various people concerning their decisions to remain unmarried. A suitable lifestyle for some people would be a very lonely life for many others.

Loneliness

I don't want to be alone
For the rest of my life.
Going to search high and low
For a good and caring wife.

A man needs a woman
For reasons on end.
Someone to come home to,
Someone to be a friend.

We always need people
Or someone to be around.
Loneliness is not a good thing,
It tends to bring us down.

When you need a shoulder
To lean or cry on,
The one you can always depend
Is the one you stay with at home.

—J. D. Jackson

Inspiration

The early years of our childhood as we searched for a body of cool water in which to go swimming. That was long before we had knowledge of lakes and pools.

Skinny Dipping

The temperature is now getting high.
And you've got time on your hands.
You can't get down to the beach,
So forget about playing in the sand.

Your mom may have a job or two
Planned for later in the day.
You need to hurry the plans you made
To cool off in the best possible way.

Out here you may have some privacy
Near a river, a stream, or a pond.
Fun and adventure are everywhere,
But you can never tell your mom.

Your friends will agree to meet you
Out by the millstream pond,
Then everyone jumps in the water
With not a stitch of clothing on.

No one's concerned about shyness;
You're just seeking ways to have fun.
You spend your free time exploring
And always keeping on the run.

The summer months were enjoyable
For you and all of your little friends.
And the memories will last a lifetime.
You'll think of them time and again.

−J. D. Jackson

Inspiration

The natural progression of one generation to the next. How one co-called educated man can question the definition of a simple word such as "is." Laws that allow convicted criminals to escape punishment. Whatever the reason—the world as I know it appears to be upside down.

A World Upside Down

Are we witnessing signs today?
Nothing makes sense anymore.
The world has turned upside down,
It's not like it was before.

Some may call it the closet.
But many more call it shame.
They're leaving it all behind,
I'd rather not mention a name.

For those who are called to lead us
To a life which is closer to Him,
They're losing the battle with Satan,
They're committing all sorts of sin.

In the early days of the industry,
Television and movies were tame.
Now when you choose to watch it,
You see every perversion you name.

Children just need to be children
And stay out of crime's way.
For those men who father a child,
You need to be a father every day.

So where will this spiral take us
That the country is in today?
Down to the depths of Hell.
Or will the nation begin to pray?

—J. D. Jackson

Inspiration

The term may vary from one part of the country to the next. Over the years, those people from well-to-do families were at times called, "four-hundreds." Which was our way of saying–rich.

Four-Hundreds

Wasn't this to be a classless society
With no special favors for any?
Apparently some never got the word.
They isolate themselves from the many.

As we traveled around this nation
Through cities large and small.
We've seen these special communities,
Many even surrounded by a wall.

They venture outside and take our money,
Then they hide behind their gates.
It's beginning to make people wonder
If we're just something they tolerate.

They used to be called four-hundreds
If they were better off than the rest.
Many of them wouldn't even socialize,
Because we could never pass their test.

Biologically speaking, we're all the same.
It's our minds that make us different.
And from the mind we get our ambitions,
Not everyone will end up affluent.

So why don't you drop this attitude
That your group is better than mine.
We're all equal in the eyes of God,
We're all just one of a kind.

—J. D. Jackson

Inspiration

My brother and a baseball player named Mickey Mantle. Both developed the symptoms of Hepatitis; both received a transplant at the same hospital. And shortly thereafter, both were diagnosed with cancer and both soon died from the horrible effects of the disease.

Brothers in Pain

There were two average American men
Who were destined to meet one day.
Although their ages were decades apart,
They never expected to meet this way.

One of them became a home run slugger
Who would play all over the land.
And when he stepped up to home plate,
The outfield showed respect for the man.

A brother was sent to help fight a war
And came back a different soul.
He had no problem readjusting to life,
But his health slowly took its toll.

Mickey Mantle was the baseball player,
And played about everywhere.
While Gene chose to help women out,
As a stylist standing behind a chair.

They were to become equals one day
Because the illness in each was the same.
Hepatitis and Cancer was not their friend,
And would take them in spite of their name.

Transplants and treatment were sure to fail
As the disease slowly took their life.
Mickey died first with family by his side,
And Gene being held by his wife.

Personal Memories and Notes

The two had become brothers in pain
As a result of some dreaded disease.
And now they can walk pain free
Their bodies are finally at ease.

—J. D. Jackson

Inspiration

A wish for everyone—Just be happy at what you choose to do, whom you're with, and where you are living. Life is so short—leave the anger behind you.

Be Happy

If you're ready to leave school
To start looking for a job to do.
Be sure to choose the right field
That's fun and enjoyable for you.

And when you begin to search
For that special lady of yours,
It's okay to be real particular
But do your share of the chores.

A few of the tricks to get you there
Is to keep a slow and steady pace.
Always be happy at what you do
And keep a smile on your face.

Has there ever been such a time
You went shopping with your wife,
And you wanted to tell a cashier
They need a change in their life?

It takes time and lots of practice
For some people to win the race.
If you want to reach the finish line,
Just keep a smile on your face.

Try to be happy when you wake up
And stay happy throughout the day.
If anger starts to creep into your life,
Start smiling and it'll stay away.

—J. D. Jackson

Inspiration

A good and lasting marriage is rare these days but is still possible. If you're not sure of each other, why marry at all? Take some time. Get to know each other. Your lives will be so much happier for the time well spent.

The Secret

It's always sad when a marriage breaks up,
Especially when there are kids involved.
The purpose of a real good courtship
Is to try and get your problems resolved.

Two young people agree to marry
Until death do they part.
Then why are there so many divorces
Before the marriage has a good start?

Money, lack of trust, or jealousy
Will wreck a marriage any day.
If you're really thinking about leaving,
Think of the price your kids will pay.

The secret to a successful marriage
Is a gift from heaven above.
And if you really want the answer,
That gift from God was love.

When uncertainty enters your marriage,
Let love be your guide.
And if frustrations rule your actions,
Remember the love and take it in stride.

—J. D. Jackson

Inspiration

All the years that Bob Hope sacrificed his own personal life for the troops wherever they were at the time. He led many USO shows here in the USA and other far off locations while his family did without his companionship. The nation owes him thanks many times over.

A Celebration of Hope

As movie celebrities come and go,
Many aren't worth a dime.
It seems that every generation or two,
A few will give of their time.

There may be a skeleton in their closet,
None of which are known by us.
They were happy to entertain the people
Without all of the fits and the fuss.

Jimmy Stewart was on the scene
With barely a word or a shout.
Liberty Valence and A Wonderful Life
Are but two that will forever stand out.

Martha Raye made us laugh
And volunteered much of her life.
She did it her way up to the end,
Married late and became a new wife.

Sidney Poitier had the right stuff
And found roles that made him great.
His acting revealed his charm and style
And possibly erased some hate.

Then we have the king of them all;
The very best was saved for last.
This man came to us from England
In the not too distant past.

Personal Memories and Notes

Bob Hope was born to entertain us.
He could act, sing and dance.
The troops will always remember him.
He entertained every available chance.

I remember him ending his shows
With a particular song, if you please.
Every American should join in and say:
Bob-We thank you-for the memories.

—J. D. Jackson

Inspiration

The various acts performed by John Walker Lindh, Jane Fonda, and all the others who for one reason or another turned against the country they call home. Whether it's money, hate, stupidity, or love for another country, traitors and deserters end up hurting us in one way or another.

Traitors and Deserters

Every great nation has its traitors,
And America has had her share.
Why they do these cowardly deeds,
Most Americans are simply not aware.

Benedict Arnold served us gallantly
During our Revolutionary War.
But then he plotted to betray us and
Deserted to the British forevermore.

Eddie Slovik was not soldier material
And, as a thief, he'd been in the joint.
Convicted of desertion in World War II,
He was shot just to make a point.

It was during the Vietnam Conflict
That Jane Fonda needed some attention.
So she went straight into the enemy camp
And showed America her real intentions.

Whether to embarrass or a religious calling,
John Walker Lindh joined with his brothers.
Since the jury is currently out on this one,
Time will decide if he joins the others.

Whether it's loyalty, greed, or stupidity,
Some Americans will betray our homeland.
Punishment should await each of them
For the damage caused by their hand.

—J. D. Jackson

Inspiration

The past is the past and we should and have learned some lessons from it. The Bible teaches us that we are not responsible for the sins of our fathers. We must always remember and learn from the past so that it is not repeated; otherwise, let it go.

Don't Call Me Brother, Brother

We're not always one happy family,
We're usually split and torn apart.
But when you sit and read the history,
Our intentions were good from the start.

No one ever argues with a dictator
Out of fear of being shot.
But a democracy is a different story.
A yes or no, they can like it or not.

This nation will stand if we're united
And will fall when we start to break up.
The signs may be pointing to a race war
Unless the doors to the past are shut.

We are not responsible for the sins
Our ancestors committed in the past.
So unless the doors are eventually closed,
This nation will probably never last.

So don't call me brother, brother
Until the family you're ready to join.
America is the world's last best hope.
And we the people decide where it's going.

—J. D. Jackson

Inspiration

One-sided breakups. Those in which the other party never had a clue about what the other one was up to.

I Don't Know Why

I don't know why you left me,
And I don't know what to say.
I still need a real good reason,
To get through one more day.

Things were always working.
You were happy when I saw you.
Then one day you packed your bags
And I didn't know what to do.

You never gave me a warning,
And you never gave me a clue.
While I was out working one day,
Someone was taking care of you.

Never take your wife for granted.
And always do the best you can.
Then tell her that you love her
And pray you're her only man.

—J. D. Jackson

Inspiration

What used to be reserved for marriage now occurs at a younger and younger age. Society no longer looks at the pregnancy of an unmarried child or woman the same way. The message they receive is that it is now okay to do what you are doing. Some mothers even go so far as to provide them with the pill. With out of control abortions and a blind eye, it's now considered a rite of passage. How sad.

Loss of Innocence

As two kids walked home after school,
Their conversation turned to a friend.
Since her mom and dad were both at work,
She asked him if he'd like to come in.

Their friend had been planning a party,
So they discussed their chances of going.
Care for a snack before you have to leave?
Better not, my mom has a way of knowing.

The night was warm; the party was a bore,
So they left and he held her hand.
As they wondered about the summer ahead,
They knew they had to make a plan.

They had been close for a couple of years,
Since they met in their new school.
As a way of celebrating the summer ahead,
He stole a kiss, breaking his own little rule.

Their parents allowed them to go off to camp,
They took this to be a good omen.
And the very first night that they were alone.
The young girl was to become a woman.

—J. D. Jackson

Inspiration

How a life of sin produces **nothing** good. And how a life can change when the need, desire, and God are there.

Hell Satan

Satan pushed me over the edge,
And I've been falling ever since.
He said he would always be there.
He's helped me clear every fence.

I was having some trouble in school
So he showed me how to lie and cheat.
He knew I was trying to join the team,
So he showed me who I had to beat.

Later in life, he knew I needed money,
So he taught me how to rob and steal.
I knew that I'd really hit the big time,
When I was hired to burn down a mill.

He told me I'd never have to worry,
And that I would never have to think.
So why is it the more he does for me,
The lower I tend to sink?

One day I remembered the fun I had
When I went to church as a kid.
Everything there was open and free,
And nothing ever had to be hid.

So I dragged myself to church one day
And I listened to the man preach.
As the Holy Ghost did His work on me,
My salvation was now in reach.

Personal Memories and Notes

Poetic Justice

I slowly turned my life around
By finding myself a new job.
I eventually had a wife and family
And have lost my desire to rob.

In spite of my troubles and wicked past,
When I would rob with a gun or knife,
I'm now looking at a brighter future
And am confident of eternal life.

—J. D. Jackson

Inspiration

Robbers, punks, hoodlums and thugs are responsible for this one. After many conversations with these people, it's so easy to see how they get trapped into a particular lifestyle. Even when given the opportunity, many of them refuse to leave it. The funny thing is, it's never their fault. If you could ask them, you would discover that someone else caused them to be locked behind bars. It has nothing to do with any action performed by them.

Hoodlums and Thugs

Every generation has had them
And ours is no exception.
For those working to be one,
To win a fight is their election.

They usually start with the weak
And slowly graduate to the others.
Nothing ever matters to them.
They even steal from their mothers.

Hoodlums and thugs have no conscience,
And I question the existence of a soul.
They will rob, steal, maim, and kill
The weak, the strong and the old.

Not being happy with the petty things,
They advance to drugs and cars.
They run around acting so big and such,
Until the cops put them behind bars.

The bars of prison won't deter them.
You're nobody till you've served time.
Yes, a few may have learned a lesson,
But most will return to their kind.

Hoodlums and thugs are Satan's children,
And are always doing work for him.
Unless they can find a quick way out,
They will die in a life of sin.

—J. D. Jackson

Inspiration

The sudden death of a colleague. This piece was written specifically for the family.

Our Last Farewell

We reported to work on Wednesday.
It was the start of a beautiful day.
This time some bad news awaited us.
We learned a colleague had passed away.

An eerie hush came over the gathering.
Then our voices soon filled the room.
What has happened to our friend?
Will all the news be given real soon?

Death is not our favorite subject.
It's not a topic we like to hear.
A number of us won't even discuss it.
If understood there's nothing to fear.

Our friend is now with his Father.
And his suffering has finally passed.
We're the ones who continue to live
And our suffering will also last.

Our condolences go out to the family.
And you must know he did his best.
Now you should rejoice in knowing
That your loved one is now at rest.

–J. D. Jackson

Inspiration

Based on the news releases concerning the people who prey on others. When you take the time to check the public records, you will find that they are not receiving suitable punishment for their crimes. The only sure way to stop the madness is for the parents to take control. Keep both eyes on your children, because the predator will not change.

The Predator

Why do you cry so, little girl?
Here, wipe away all those tears.
I don't remember seeing you before,
And I've been coming here for years.

Come now, sit down here beside me.
It's all right; you don't have to be afraid.
Can you tell me where your mom is?
What's your age? What's your grade?

Listen, are you feeling all right now?
Oh! By the way, my name is Ron.
Get in my car and I'll take you home.
No, don't do that, I want my mom.

Why do you cry so, young man?
Here, wipe away all those tears.
I don't remember seeing you before,
And I've been coming here for years.

—J. D. Jackson

Inspiration

Every last baby boomer of my generation. The times we have had and the contributions we have made to the world. Many of them good and some that don't deserve mention.

Baby Boomers

The war in Europe was over now,
And the men were coming home.
Adjustments were made all over,
And wives were no longer alone.

From the horrors of the world war
And from a land that was war torn,
Normalcy was creeping back home.
Millions of babies were being born.

If each one could tell their own story,
There's so much that each could say.
As one of the very early boomers
I was born on a hot summer day.

The boomers started to enjoy life
During the last years of the fifties.
We came of age and will never forget
The decade of the nineteen sixties.

Over the years we've seen electronics
Go from hot tubes, transistors to chips.
We advanced flight from the propjets
To landing on the moon in a space ship.

We've witnessed so many new advances,
From televisions, computers and more.
They've made many changes in the world,
And they've opened so many new doors.

Personal Memories and Notes

Consider the things that you've witnessed.
The advancements, victories, and cheers.
Is there anything you'd like to eliminate?
Can you do without all the tears?

The boomers will be facing their twilight
In just a few years from now.
Can you imagine the sights they've seen?
Can you imagine what's coming down?

—J. D. Jackson

Inspiration

Every woman's wedding day. May it be everything you want it to be.

My Wedding Day

This is beginning to look like
The happiest day of my life.
In just a few hours from now,
I'll be married-I'll be a wife.

I've looked forward to this day
With so much anticipation.
The way things are looking now,
It will surpass my expectations.

Every bride has surely dreamed
Of a perfect wedding day.
All the plans are double-checked,
And her fears are held at bay.

My wedding day has finally arrived.
In a moment I'll become a wife.
And as we stand before our God,
I look forward to my new life.

I'll remember this day for a lifetime.
They'll be no tears except for joy.
He treats me with love and respect,
And not like a grown man's toy.

If the future brings me sorrow,
I'll reflect back on this day.
I'll try to remember our happiness,
And I'll wish the pain away.

—J. D. Jackson

Inspiration

To those who don't quite get it. To the blondes and to those of us who get it five minutes after everyone else. A piece of humor.

Anybody Home?

How many times does it have to rain
Before the message you finally get?
When you come in from the outside,
Are your clothes always wet?

Don't ever argue with your parents.
Remember they've been in your shoes,
And they know the tricks you're up to
Because they've already paid their dues.

Don't always look for the obvious,
If your mate is messing around.
His reputation may be solid,
Because his affairs are out of town.

When you set your sights on a lady,
And she takes a liking to you.
As your relationship begins taking off,
A no doesn't mean—continue.

Know where to look for the answers,
They're not always under your nose.
Patience, common sense and courtesy
Will open doors where anything goes.

—J. D. Jackson

Inspiration

Troubles in general. Trouble getting up, trouble getting to sleep, trouble at work, trouble at home, trouble with the traffic, troubles in the world, etc. Everyone seems to have them and if we don't find a way to handle them, they will find a way to handle us.

You Think You Got Troubles

Trouble seems to follow us everywhere we go.
For some misguided people, trouble is all they know.
Even when we try to do the things we know are right;
Trouble will always find us any old day or night.

People have troubles like none they've seen before.
And as soon as they awake, trouble is at their door.
Trouble has a way of following some kids to school,
But on the positive side, they learn the golden rule.

There are so many troubles in this world today.
Like finding a girl that'll care enough to stay.
Can't raise a child because troubles are so great.
Because of troubles, people learn how to take.

There are so many troubles to take care of at home.
A man leaves his family and now they're all alone.
Troubles have a way of keeping us on our toes.
And when facing your own troubles, anything goes.

Troubles, for some, have become a way of life.
Troubles can't discern between a man and wife.
If we learn to handle troubles just one at a time,
Our lives should turn out great-yours and mine.

–J. D. Jackson

Inspiration

The two of us. It's been a good life for us and we've had lots of fun. Even though we're headed down hill, age wise, we still have some good years left and will continue to have fun. Life is good.

Old Man — Old Woman

Now wasn't that nice the way that lady talked to me?
Apparently there's more here than you can possibly see.
If you don't behave yourself, I'm going to show you my boot.
You need to bring yourself back down to earth you old coot.

What in heaven's name is going through your little mind?
Do you think I really care if that thing is one of a kind?
What would you expect me to do if it were to fall over on you?
With a Harley that size, there is nothing I could possibly do.

I thought we had this same discussion about twenty years ago.
For you to make it this far, there are things you had to know.
Don't you understand that age creeps up on people like you,
And there are certain things in life your body can no longer do?

So what if you are hearing about Viagra all over town?
You try one or two and I'll be putting you in the ground.
What do you mean, you're going to try that new hair drug?
If you're trying to look sixty-five again, just buy a new rug.

Heaven's bells, couldn't you find something else to hide?
You know you have to wear your teeth when you go outside.
Some days I feel as if I've received the ultimate curse.
But then I believe the preacher did say, for better or worse.

The Lord knows we've had our good days and bad,
But there's nothing I'd trade for all that I've had.
You just keep on doing those crazy things you do
And as long as I am alive—I'll just keep on loving you.

−J. D. Jackson

Inspiration

Our children, grandchildren and children around the world. The potential in these kids is unlimited and it's our job as adults to love and take care of them. So love them, listen to them, and correct them along the way. As with the mind, a child is a terrible thing to waste. Let them be children and let them enjoy life.

The Baby

I saw a newborn baby
It was full of beauty and charm.
People standing around him,
Checking fingers, toes, and arms.

I quietly asked myself
Looking twenty years ahead.
Would we change thing's now
If we found that he was dead?

We always have to remember
That children depend upon us.
And their success or failure
Was placed in our trust.

If a pup has no direction,
It tends to run around wild.
So when all the charm is gone,
Give direction to your child.

Each and every last child
Needs our love and devotion.
So always try and be there,
When they start a commotion.

A child has so much potential,
And may be physical or smart.
If you bring yours up properly,
From God they'll never part.

—J. D. Jackson

Inspiration

Fear. Fear of the unknown does cause us great concern. The thing's that are going on around this lady should give each one of us something to think about. You never know who or what may be lurking just outside your window, do you? In this case, she found out too late. Be prepared.

Sounds

There—I heard it again.
Never heard it before—it was an odd sound.
He knew I was scared.
Even if his work is important—why leave now?

Can't seem to get settled.
I've taken my bath—I've even tried to read.
It just doesn't feel right.
He left me his number—I have what I need.

What was that?
I've checked all around the front—the side.
I love this house,
But I can't think of a safe place to go and hide.

Stop it—who's there?
I knew we should have bought that gun.
Who am I kidding?
Even if I saw someone—which one would run?

What are those sounds?
I've heard about all I plan to take.
What's going on?
I have to walk around—I have to stay awake.

Should I call someone?
Sure. Then everyone will know that I'm crazy.
One more sound—I'm gone.
What was that? Nooooooooooooooo!

—J. D. Jackson

Inspiration

One of the events most of us never want to see or think about: Death. It's inevitable, so why shouldn't we think or talk about it sometime? Proper preparation can make it much easier to face. Proper preparation can ease the financial burdens that some families must face. If you're a believer, death is just the beginning.

Death

As a child it's okay to play and have fun.
We adults have had our share.
But always remember when to draw the line
And never accept the wrong dare.

When it's time to leave our childhood behind,
We'll make decisions about life ahead.
It's smart to consider the choices we make.
Do we work or go to college instead?

As adults we'll have many challenges to face
And new ones will hit us each day.
But if we always do what we know is right,
From the path we'll never stray.

And the closer we get to the age of fifty,
Our daily routine seems to change.
The body can't keep up with the brain anymore
And our activities now have a range.

Most of us will worry about tomorrow,
And we reflect back on things we've done.
As the years continue to pass slowly by,
From death we will constantly run.

We have one chance to live our lives.
We struggle as we learn what it's about.
But death will come to you and me—
About that, there is no doubt.

—J. D. Jackson

Inspiration

A subject that has been on my mind for quite some time now, one of the three unalienable rights given us and mentioned in the Declaration of Independence. And that's our right to **pursuit of Happiness**. According to the proper definition of the word unalienable, and as it is used in this document, it is from God and therefore cannot be given or taken away by man. That being the case, then why do the states continue to do just that? Makes you wonder, doesn't it?

Pursuit of Happiness

From the document that declared us a nation,
Comes a phrase very few ever discuss.
Being clearly stated by our forefathers,
Was a right God bestowed upon us.

Each person pursues his own happiness
Based on their life, which lies ahead.
With so many decisions to be made,
Will it be happiness or career instead?

If you end up making the right choice,
You'll get two for the price of one.
Because your happiness is in what you do,
Some of our choices can also be fun.

Money tends to make people happy.
It can also cause problems galore.
Used properly, it'll answer many prayers.
If not, it'll create even more.

Our pursuit of happiness is relentless.
It keeps us active day after day.
For some, happiness is a certain person
For others, it's a special place to stay.

We choose our own level of happiness.
We choose where it is we stay.
So where does a government get the right
Through annexation to take it away?

—J. D. Jackson

Inspiration

People pray, there's no doubt about that. When you feel the need, do it. But don't ever forget to give Him the praise. In spite of what some people may think, He is responsible for everything here on earth. Praise Him.

Give God the Praise

Talk to God when you need Him
And pray to Him every day.
He wants to hear from each of us
And He'll listen to what we say.

If you'll knock, His door will open.
If you ask, you shall receive.
He'll answer each of our prayers.
In Him, you can trust and believe.

No need to worry about tomorrow
If you always rely upon Him.
But those who live for Satan
Will always blame and condemn.

Let's give God the praise and glory
For what He's done for you and me.
If He's always in your heart,
Non-believers will begin to see.

Why do some of the most educated
Trust only the things they can see?
And many others say convincingly
From the ocean we came to be.

It's so easy to believe in Darwin
Or to awake and say it's not so.
But then on the day of judgement
Where is it you plan to go?

—J. D. Jackson

Inspiration

The total loss of one's family. How would you handle it? Most of us don't ever want to think of the possibility of going through that. This particular individual couldn't stand the pain and ended up turning to the bottle. The abuse of alcohol eventually led him into a life of sin.

Life of Sin

As the haze burned off this morning
And the birds were busy at play,
I sat on this bench and I wondered
Just how to get through another day.

At times my pain is too unbearable
As I think of what used to be.
I remember waking up each morning
With you looking back at me.

As our plans began to unfold,
A true blessing was given us two—
A beautiful little bundle of joy
Whose features looked exactly like you.

The weather was hot and sunny
As you returned from the lake that day.
And the reasons I had for living
Were so tragically taken away.

I mourned my loss for a year or more
As I tried to carry on with my life.
But all the things were missing now
Which were provided by my baby and wife.

So I slowly turned to the bottle
To mask the pain I have within.
Although I have fleeting moments,
There's no escape from this life of sin.

—J. D. Jackson

Inspiration

Why some people in our society accept prison life as the good life. Many of those who are eventually released do not hesitate to commit another crime so that they can return to prison. Most of what they need or want out of life is provided them, for the most part, free of charge. They can receive a four-year or numerous associate degrees at little or no expense to them. Free medical and dental, except for a minor co-pay fee, and that includes major operations. On top of that, as soon as anything happens that they don't like, a lawsuit is filed against the state. For a good portion of today's inmate population, prison life is the good life.

The Good Life

They're headed down the chute
And eyes are everywhere.
Going down to have some lunch,
Trying hard to avoid the stare.

Cons just looking for a chance
To stop and make a deal.
In the joint, where anything goes,
Make sure you never squeal.

The life of a convict is boring,
Until you learn to play the game.
Compared to life on the outside,
In the joint it's really tame.

Don't have to worry about a drive-by,
And my education is free.
If I should fall while trying to escape,
They'll repair or replace my knee.

Why do bad things always happen
To a good man such as me?
I've tried so hard all my life
To be the best crook that I could be.

But then I think of the fun I'll have
As I prepare to leave the gate.
Can't think of all the things I'll do
With the money I sued from the state.

—J. D. Jackson

Inspiration

Childhood memories inspired this one. I've listed good memories first, what society has become, and then one possible solution. You have memories too, some good, some bad. Think about them sometime, they might make you smile.

Days of Long Ago

Give me those long hot summer days
To work and play about.
Oh, how I enjoyed walking the woods
Where no one could hear a shout.

I miss those sweet days of long ago.
We had not a care in the world.
The best thing to do on a Saturday night
Was to date your steady girl.

But now it seems that evil has won,
With crime still on the spread.
And if you choose to sit on the porch,
You're likely to end up dead.

How do we take back that which is ours
So we can enjoy our life again?
Build the prisons and punish those guilty
Of committing all the sin.

−J. D. Jackson

0-595-23508-5

Printed in the United States
101419LV00006B/37/A